# RUN OUT OF PROSE

# MARVIN COHEN

© 2018 by Marvin Cohen

All Rights Reserved.

Set in Trump Mediaeval with LaTeX.

ISBN: 978-1-944697-64-8 (paperback)
ISBN: 978-1-944697-65-5 (ebook)
Library of Congress Control Number: 2018932977

Sagging Meniscus Press
saggingmeniscus.com

# Contents

| | |
|---|---|
| AUTHOR BESEECHES PUBLISHER, WHO'S CAUTIOUS | 1 |
| A MUTUALLY NECESSARY PAIR | 2 |
| SLEEP TOO SLUGGISH TO COME TO THE RESCUE OF ITS PONDEROUS SELF-LACK | 4 |
| HINTS TO MAKE GOOD USE OF OUR PERSONAL BODIES | 5 |
| THE TOTAL REPLACEMENT BY DEATH OF LIFE | 6 |
| LOVE? WHAT HAPPENED? | 7 |
| WHAT ABOUT THE FRIENDLY WORLD, SO TO SPEAK? | 8 |
| HIS ONLY DEATH, AND I'M ONLY ME | 11 |
| DEATH IS MORE RADICAL THAN LIFE | 12 |
| COMPETITIVE MOTIVATION: A LECTURE | 13 |
| ESSENTIALS UNDER DISCUSSION | 14 |
| AN UNDETAILED ACCOUNT OF LIFE | 16 |
| THE PERMANENT INTERRUPTION | 17 |
| NO TIME LEFT: THE WORST HAS ARRIVED | 18 |
| BEARING A CAUTIOUS ATTITUDE TO WHAT YOU WANT | 20 |
| HOW "NOTHING" STANDS IN THE WAY | 21 |
| BEING CAREFUL | 22 |
| JANE AUSTEN'S CENSORED ENGLISH TRAGEDY | 24 |
| ASKING FOR TOO MUCH? I HOPE NOT | 26 |

| | |
|---|---|
| SOME RUDE COUNSEL | 28 |
| TIME'S PERMISSION TO BE LIVE ONCE | 29 |
| AL, GONE | 30 |
| INTERSPECIES MUTUAL SAFETY | 31 |
| I PLACE THE BIRDS ON A LOFTY PEDESTAL | 32 |
| REMINISCENCES FROM A NEARLY DRAINED UP GLASS | 33 |
| SUBWAY PORNOGRAPHY | 34 |
| BETTER LINKED FOR KEEPING APART | 35 |
| TIME'S INFIDELITY TO ITSELF | 36 |
| ASPECTS OF OUR KIND | 37 |
| SOME MARRIAGES STAY | 38 |
| PROVISIONAL QUESTIONS | 39 |
| EVEN IF YOU PERSONALLY DON'T CONTRIBUTE, YOU'RE BOUND TO BE A BENEFICIARY OF EVOLUTION, WITH ENOUGH LARGESS TO SUPPORT US ALL | 40 |
| A WORD BOND FRAYED. (IT'S TRUE, I'M AFRAID) | 42 |
| SORRY, READERSHIP | 44 |
| WHAT IS LIFE FROM THE INSIDE? | 45 |
| KEEPING THINGS GOING | 46 |
| THE BIRD ASSAULT | 47 |
| WHAT WE ALWAYS HAVE, UNLESS DEMENTIA COMES | 48 |
| THE EMOTIONAL LIFE, FULL OF FEELING | 50 |
| THE MYSTIQUE OF RELATIONSHIPS | 52 |
| TO BE HAPPY, GET MISERABLE FIRST | 53 |
| COMPARING THE PAIR | 54 |

| | |
|---|---|
| EVOLUTION DOESN'T NEED MY PRAISE, BUT HERE GOES | 55 |
| THERE'S VIRTUALLY ENOUGH TIME FOR ANYTHING, ALMOST | 56 |
| ALLOTMENT OF CREDIT: ENGLAND'S REWARD | 57 |
| PASSABLY EASIER | 58 |
| THE CONFUSION THAT BLENDS IN AT THE RIGHT TIME | 59 |
| WHAT TO DO, JUST IN CASE | 60 |
| THE PRIVILEGED WOMAN WHO STILL WORRIES | 61 |
| MARRIAGE CYCLE (in 4 parts) | 62 |
| THE LONG, NEEDY PROCESS AND ITS SURPRISINGLY ABRUPT END | 64 |
| HOW TO TAKE OR NOT TAKE THAT MYSTERY CALLED "LIFE" | 65 |
| PHILOSOPHY'S BEARING ON LIFE ITSELF, BY WAY OF INSIDE STRATEGY | 66 |
| LET THE GOING THING GO ON | 67 |
| A LITERARY METAPHOR FOR SEXUAL NON-FULFILLINGNESS | 68 |
| ANTI-THEATRICS | 69 |
| A TRIO OF OUR LOVE | 70 |
| THE LIFE SCIENCE DEPARTMENT'S INADEQUATE PSEUDO BIOLOGY'S FRAUDULENT PROFESSOR IS SUPPOSED TO TEACH DARWIN | 72 |
| A LOFTY, YET EARTHLY, COMPARISON | 74 |
| A PERSONAL PLEA TO THE PRESS | 75 |
| THE WAITER SAVES THE DAY | 76 |
| THE HENCE & THE WHENCE | 77 |
| EVOLUTION INTRIGUES | 78 |

| | |
|---|---|
| PRESERVING RETAINED FADING MEMORY BLOSSOMS | 80 |
| PUBLICATION'S FAILURE PROJECT | 81 |
| CONTEMPLATING THE QUINTESSENTIAL ESSENCE | 82 |
| THAT OLD TANTALIZING SEARCH | 83 |
| POLITICALLY ANGRY | 84 |
| CURIOSITY GETS FATIGUED | 87 |
| THE SAINT, ALMOST | 88 |
| DEFENDING DARWIN'S FAME (BUT I'M NOT A LAWYER) | 90 |
| CAPACITY | 92 |
| KEEP UP OUR COLLECTIVE GOING ON | 93 |
| CREATING VIA ORIGINALITY | 94 |
| THE WHOLE THING. WHAT IS IT? | 95 |
| OUR UNIQUE TWO-WAY WORLD LANDLORD | 96 |
| THOSE TWO ENDS OF THE UNIVERSE | 97 |
| HOW INTELLECTUALLY TO TRANSCEND WHAT YOU DEPARTED FROM | 98 |
| TWO JIMMY POEMS | 100 |
| IS A VERY OLD MAN'S ERECTION LIKE A STERILE STILL-BIRTH THAT PRODUCES NOT EVEN A BABY'S GHOST? | 101 |
| LIFE AT ITS EXCESS POINTS, WHERE CORRELATIVES COME INTO PLAY, TO PRODUCE A SANITY-CONDUCIVE BLUEPRINT | 102 |
| THE EARLIER–LATER TESTS BY ONESELF ON ONESELF IN LIVING EXPERIENCE | 104 |
| WOMEN'S DISTINGUISHED LOSS | 105 |
| IT'S EITHER ROUND THEY GO, OR NOTHING AT ALL | 106 |

| | |
|---|---|
| HOW TO LET ASTRONOMY PROTECT YOUR LAZINESS | 108 |
| TWO VIEWS OF THE WORLD, INCLUDING SELF | 110 |
| I WIN BY A STONE'S THROW | 112 |
| FARMING THE OBVIOUS, RISKING UNPOPULARITY THEREBY | 114 |
| WHAT AT FIRST SEEMED LIKE DESPERATE ACTION TURNS UNNECESSARY | 116 |
| ADVICE TO CONSTANTLY TAKE | 118 |
| MOODS AND STOMACHS | 120 |
| TURN-TAKING: THE ART OF DISPLACING ME | 122 |
| WHAT HAS ESCAPE RESCUED ME FROM, IF IT DID? AFTER HAVING UNDERGONE WHAT? | 124 |
| A SOCIAL COMPLAINT, THEN A PRIVATE DENIAL | 126 |
| HISTORY'S SECRETED HUSH-HUSH ON THE WAY OVER | 127 |
| A MECHANICAL FAILURE | 128 |
| THE MISPLACED WRITER IN A NEW ERA | 129 |
| A SELF-DESCRIPTION | 130 |
| FINAL LEAKS FROM THE INK-JOWLED PEN, PRE-COMPUTER STYLE | 132 |
| FAMILIARITY WITHIN AN UNEASY DWELLING PLACE | 134 |
| A LOAD OF FREE ADVICE | 135 |
| INCENTIVE FOR ACTIVISM | 136 |
| SAYING MORE THAN I CAN THINK | 138 |
| ADVICE TO APPLY. TRY IT. | 140 |
| A PARABLE THAT CAN'T FIND ITSELF | 141 |
| WHAT WE'RE IN FOR | 142 |

| | |
|---|---|
| ABSTRACT TO THE CORE | 144 |
| SUSPENDED WORDS SLOWLY THAWING ON A HOLIDAY CRUISE | 146 |
| A COLLECTION OF UNCERTAIN RECOLLECTIONS, CATEGORICALLY DISORGANIZED | 148 |
| LIFE'S TWISTY RHYTHMS | 150 |
| A MAN'S MANIFESTO | 153 |
| STUDIES IN HUMAN RIVALRY | 154 |
| NOTES ON HOW HUMANS MAKE USE OF THE EARTH, OR NOT | 156 |
| THE GOODS AND BADS OF EVOLUTION | 157 |
| THE HEEDLESS WORLD LEAVES ME BEHIND | 158 |
| YES, BUT | 160 |
| THE UNDERSTUDY ROLE? NO! | 161 |
| PROLONG YOUR STAY | 162 |
| FEAR OF CROWDS | 164 |
| FEATURES AND PROBLEMS | 165 |
| A PRETTY STRANGER EXERCISES HER RIGHT TO REJECT YOU | 166 |
| A SEA CATASTROPHE AS A MASS GRAVE FOR THE HUMAN RACE | 168 |
| PROBLEM DIALOGUE | 169 |
| POETRY DIALOGUE | 170 |
| PATENT DIALOGUE | 171 |
| MEMORY DIALOGUE | 172 |
| THE OPPORTUNITIES OF DONE DUTIES | 174 |
| THE MAJOR MATTER, NO MATTER WHAT | 175 |
| INSOLUBLE | 176 |
| EVOLUTION VERSUS CIVILIZATION | 177 |

| KEEP GOING | 178 |
| WHAT I OWE DARWIN | 179 |
| WHY RELIGION TAKES THE SCARE OUT OF LIFE | 180 |
| BRING IN A PRIEST | 181 |
| DEITY'S DESPERATE NEED | 182 |
| A CLERGY MARKET | 183 |
| UNCAGED, LOOK FOR DEMOCRATIC FREEDOM | 184 |
| SELF-PROTECTION | 185 |
| NUGGETS FROM LIFE'S WISDOM | 186 |
| DECORUM | 187 |
| NAIVETÉ IN ACTION | 188 |
| HOW TO PREPARE | 189 |
| A DUBIOUS ADVERTISEMENT FOR COUNTRY LIVING | 190 |
| THE WORLD AS OUR LANDLORD. BENEVOLENT? NOT ALWAYS | 192 |
| THE SWOON OF THE SELF-LOST | 194 |
| NO TRANSLATION | 195 |
| GIVE UP? SHAME ON YOU | 196 |
| HURRY UP TO STOP | 197 |
| DIPPING AND DROWNING IN THE SEA OF OTHERS | 198 |
| ADDRESS TOPIC: HOW DOES THE WORLD FARE? | 200 |
| THE PUBLIC'S VERDICT—IS THAT WHAT LIFE COMES DOWN OR UP TO? | 202 |
| WHY THE NOW AND THEN IS PREFERABLE TO THE ALL AT ONCE | 203 |
| UNCOMFORTABLE. (THE RIGHT TO BE SHY) | 204 |
| THE TUNE-LADEN BIRD | 205 |

| | |
|---|---|
| ALL ABOUT MOST EVERYTHING, JUST ABOUT | 206 |
| THIS WAS ACTUALLY BROADCAST? | 208 |
| BOASTING TOWARD ADMIRATION | 209 |
| AMBITION'S SOCIAL ULTIMATE | 210 |
| MUTUAL CURE | 211 |
| MARITAL DISPUTE APPEASED | 212 |
| TERM IT TRAGEDY TO FORCE BLAME OUT | 213 |
| TWO OLD CELEBRITIES | 214 |
| THE UNTIRING FLAVOR OF A WORD FAVORITE | 216 |
| THE CURATIVE ANESTHESIA | 217 |
| *A Tribute to M.C., by Peter Jackson* | 218 |

# Run Out of Prose

# AUTHOR BESEECHES PUBLISHER, WHO'S CAUTIOUS

"It begs to be published,"
the author fervently said.
"But you're not its author yet,
till I give the go-ahead,
to see it through into print.
So first I must read it yet,
to authorize that you're its author,
and not a mere manuscript submitter
who if I reject it, would turn bitter."

# A MUTUALLY NECESSARY PAIR

1.

Geography is the eye of history:
you must visualize
in order to surmise.
Is that any mystery?

2.

You see things flying by.
Just where do they transpire?
To conceive of the whole entire,
just fit the "when" to your searching eye.

3.

Give geography a chance
to match "French Revolution" under "France."

4.

"When" and "where" are a mating couple.
They jointly unpuzzle the muddled trouble
of understanding's ill-balanced bubble
that threatens to join the neighboring rubble
like a shave turned back into its old stubble.

5.

(But don't forget the "who" and "what."
Add also the quizzical "why."
Thus the plot thickens, by and by,
as connections crumble into their original dot.
All together, shout "that's a lot!"
What's left? Insert in the slot
an unneeded match to the already boiled pot.)

## SLEEP TOO SLUGGISH TO COME TO THE RESCUE OF ITS PONDEROUS SELF-LACK

There's a yawning gulf between the sleep I need and the sleep I get. This yawning gulf pries my mouth apart and stiffens the corners, till fatigue claps me shut. Insomnia challenges my sleeplessness to a drowsy duel, but the victor is too tired to crawl off with the prize of the sudden unconscious jolt of sleep, recognized upon awakening as something that should have prolonged itself if only it had been alert enough. That lost opportunity drags itself down the fatigue slope and splashes a pool of water on the bitter reawakening of an intense focus on its own restless resistance to Sleep: that off-center goal of consciousness surrendering to unconscious oblivion on the cradle of its own relaxation and an abandonment of curiosity's self-prying habits. I could go on about this ...

# HINTS TO MAKE GOOD USE OF OUR PERSONAL BODIES

The zones that identify gender
engender solid steady grooves to our pleasure.
Palates placed under the tongue
paint a sure brush for old or young,
opening a sluice to saliva's waterfall too,
to guide food to the consuming zoo
where hunger gets pulverized into a powder
and however tattered, the stomach must sing louder.
Don't forget urination. It gives such relief:
either whitish or yellowish, it sustains belief
that making a vacuum in the bladder
heightens the climb up enjoyment's ladder.
So here's a salute to the human body.
It contributes to our well being, oddly.

## THE TOTAL REPLACEMENT BY DEATH OF LIFE

No religious bridge can shorten the gap
between new death and good old life.
Faith is a desperate illusion.
Skeleton empties skull of the brain
necessary to imagine heaven.
Belief is a desperate failure.
God is an empty word
substituting for secular luck
in games of chance on the good old earth.
There's never been a miracle
transcendently supernatural.
People's identities stop
once death voids their good old lives.
But their lives weren't that good anyway.
Death is the ultimate negative comparison,
devastatingly catastrophic
to all that life ever built up
in the wild ecstasy of its imagination
that prays to keep itself going.

## LOVE? WHAT HAPPENED?

So if it ends badly, does that deny the good stuff earlier?
No. Wasn't the love already recorded?
It happened indelibly, borne witness by history
of our solo two. We couldn't be smashed.
"Forever" underwent a wedge of deterioration intervening
by disappointing stages inching in
and regretfully issuing out its nullity
where desire anew flamed for someone else
in our both cases. Our last act of simultaneity
confirmed that all along we belonged together.
Ironically, that's how we tossed it off
by the fierce act of rationalization.
Double betrayal, toying with the flame
that passes the sacred torch
to two new passionate newcomers
that caught our frenzy, in turn.
Thus by sadness-distribution
I regretted less, she slightly more,
both victims to time's romantic changeability
and fickle abuse of sworn fidelity.

# WHAT ABOUT THE FRIENDLY WORLD, SO TO SPEAK?

1.

I'm nothing were it not for the world
which sizzles all by itself
outside my personal layers of membrane
called by dermatologists the skin:
protective, but permeable,
the disease barrier that lets disease in,
the gatekeeper of the tides
that push and pull like a tug-of-war
between whooping-it-up warring factions
with me spinning in between
like the sensitive prize all this war is about.

2.

The world's air I breathe in by gulps,
jealous to portion out my full share
for the healthy burst of my lungs
whose elastic durability is athletic.
The wild seas of blood are kept within
by arterial conduits in neat mapping geography
conducted privately in the course of veins:
disciplined ranks like army maneuvers.

3.

The green carpet of earth spreads around;
and upward trees display their immense branches
for the sky to frolic with, blue and away,
like children celebrating momentary absences
of guardian parents in their severe ranks.
The sky spreads space around like a profligate
fooling with the toy of abundance. Thunder will ring
to hasten shouts of scared merriment.
The protected children grow up. Still scared.

4.

So here I am. Together, my world & me.
What about my fellow human beings?
Such is the science of sociality:
inward toward psychology, but outward-devised
to the grim, relentless game of politics
that rules huge multitudes and fights for the right
to distribute economic wealth in disproportionate ranks
that create the destructive force of poverty
in cruel deprivation of the worldly goods
that swell to surplus among the unembarrassed rich.

5.

Have I exhausted my catalogue of the outside world
that provides substance and opportunity
for the likes of little me to conquer and thrive
by the opportunistic deployment of ambition,
creating admiration if possible, and prestige,
to give my status such upward mobility
as to fend off the anxious insecurities of life?

6.

There's still astronomy to talk about, plus religion,
that includes myths, legends, and conventional superstition
that deifies religious celebrities
while defying the parlor game of logic.
Such delicate subjects I won't go into
for fear of offending my fellow beings' sensitivity
when opinions clash with identities in a conflicting universe.
Respectability is not to be pulled down by insult
to the core itself of where one comes from
and connective change along the route of life.
Can't we get along? That's the puzzle of it all.
We'll point the cannon guzzles, but leave the ammunition
to one side. Don't pull the malicious switch
to let the dogs of ugliness rule and snarl.

# HIS ONLY DEATH, AND I'M ONLY ME

Oh poor Al. He's dead. What a rotten thing to be.
What am I doing being alive then?
Have I betrayed him by not sharing his state?
We used to share states, but that was a lively one,
that allowed us to cement our friendship.
And a long run we had, between us.
Conversations humorous, ironic, and dire.
Consoling each other, when the consolation was needed,
especially if a girlfriend rejected one of us.
I physically shared his burden in moving
all his effects from the old to the new place.
But this time he moved to a dividing place
from which our union can never recover.
My consciousness is filled with him
in a never-ending lament.
As for him, no consciousness is left
once skull and bones emptied the flesh of itself
that bore my impress in his old memory.
The Marvin that uniquely was his
is transferred to me, as an unwanted gift.

## DEATH IS MORE RADICAL THAN LIFE

His being dead is so different
than my usual tenure of life.
What's it like, for him
not to even experience anything,
and therefore having nothing to report
to us, his still-alive fellows,
who long to hear of his vacuity
if a language could be invented for it?
The gap between us is too great
even for metaphysics to bridge.
Religion means nothing to him, nor to me,
giving us at least that in common,
but that's a small consolation,
for it brings me no closer to him,
in his unreachable capacity for death.
He's a master at it. Who am I,
lounging here, surrounded by habitual life,
where pain and joy chase each other endlessly?
However, I grow weaker toward his state,
approaching some link between the two of us
that unpolarizes our differences.
But what's the rush? My lingering
has nature and motivation to back it up
and caution's quiet conservatism.
I'm alright here. Don't bother me.

## **COMPETITIVE MOTIVATION: A LECTURE**

Publishing! said the writers,
Gallery exhibitions! said the painters,
Concert halls! said the composers,
Stages! Films! said the playwrights.
Love! said the romantic. (That's all of us.)
Goals! Goals! demanded the hockey players
brandishing their slippery pucks.
Soccer players with their endless legs
and foreheads ached for goals—
The world is goal-drunk!
Winning! Winning!
Oh, but what of failure?
Failure's one choice among the smells
is the stinkiest. Nothing less.
But losers have no choices.
Winners are all rejoicers.
Winners love to be first.
Losers hold back their tears, then burst.

## ESSENTIALS UNDER DISCUSSION

Now in my post-sex old age
I remember those olden golden days
as though when they were there, nothing else was there
but sex; but also life was included
as sex's basic essential background
so that sex would have a decent home to live in;
for where would sex be without life
to provide the organic basis of its energy,
and the wherewithal for sex to happen
in the comfort and security that life provides?
So remember: no life, no sex,
so first you must be born,
grow up, and then it's time for maturity
to harbor sex in its embryo.
First things first, of course.
We must know the source.
Then it's time to be sauce-
y. So have fun, boys and girls,
cultivate your straight hair or curls
to captivate your new-found mate.
Achieve, then, sex's normal state.
But those times will abate
when death replaces sex
and our old passion is now an ex-.

Nostalgic? Not for long.
Death ends this old song.
Where's the right, where's the wrong?
Life, sex, and song
I'll no longer prolong.
Dear readers, "So long."

# AN UNDETAILED ACCOUNT OF LIFE

As I look out upon the broad world,
I regard it as a getting-born reward
despite my helpless will playing no part in it.
The role of my personal responsibility
for the world setting its gift upon my lap
was mere pure blind acceptance,
the lucky passivity of my going along,
steered by those strangers, my parents,
fired up by the instinctive roles to play
as owners or renters of my little baby self.
I grew up, but lived so full a life
by the mechanical count of mere years,
that now, longevity's survivor,
my body falls into a preparation for death,
and not my own fault, but I have to go.
My brain has cooled down, and I'm drugged.
My verbalized thinking enters a feeble stage
and having known many people, I drift away
escorted by the blunt hand of pain.

# THE PERMANENT INTERRUPTION

Too late, now, to have any more sex.
That period in my life is now an ex.
The culprit, of course, is old age,
causing me, in life's book, to turn the page.
I'm impotent, but I'm also a sage.
My old cock is docile in its cage.
So pity me, you young folks.
I no longer produce those powerful pokes.
They're reduced to a series of jokes.
Thus my confession is pronounced.
Energy has drained out to its last ounce.
Now I sit still. I used to pounce.
Thus inevitable sadness ensues.
The song of the incurable blues.

# NO TIME LEFT: THE WORST HAS ARRIVED

1.

Old age has reduced sex to none.
Consoled by wisdom, what can replace fun?
And I'm not the only lonely one.

2.

Grown too old, I'm penalized
that my libido has been downsized
and taken away what was most prized.

3.

Goodbye, youth.
You were the true truth.
This is my pre-death salute
to my post-sex voice, now mute.

4.

Tragedy? Of course.
It's, subtle, but coarse,
to go so off course
bearing a crooked cross.

5.

On the date of its expiration
my cock yields to no temptation.
Though I was such a he-man,
girls don't magnetize my semen
to spurt their fertile juices out
to end the frenzied bout
with mixed result, no doubt.

6.

The ending in store for old men to realize,
thanks to this poem, comes as no surprise.
Did you expect eternity's sunrise?
Your barren body, empty of supplies,
says, "Settle your affairs, if you're wise,
discontinue those entangling ties,

7.

wrap passion and romance in mothballs,
reluctantly heed the carrion calls
as the solitude of demise falls
on the whole body, not just balls,
and so you enter the 'hallowed halls.'"

## BEARING A CAUTIOUS ATTITUDE TO WHAT YOU WANT

Watch out what you want.
If too desperate the want,
you suffer not getting it.
If you satisfied a want before,
don't be too sure
of making a repeat capture.
Some performances aren't guaranteed
for an automatic echo
to summon the same deliverance.
Some historical moments bear no future habit.
Once only, then off the stage
or rarely on occasion,
nostalgia procuring its own past
in an astounding rescue act,
squeezing time into itself,
defying change's tyranny
and building momentarily a monument
to a second act, permission granted
by the marvelous mechanics of chance
that randomly blesses you once
or later too, if the formula holds.

# HOW "NOTHING" STANDS IN THE WAY

Life is so precious, aren't you scared
to lose the whole grand deal, and that's it?
Preserving! and Maintaining!—
life is worth those two colossal efforts.
For, once slippery life you lose the hold of,
and it breaks lose,
only one thing replaces it: Nothing.
Doesn't "nothing" scare you?
It's known under a euphemism: Death.
Religion is helpless to modify it.
Death is supreme. To defy it, religion
tries to weave its holy magic,
but death is firm in its reality
and poor religion is left gasping at the gate,
weeping, crying, wailing,
oozing out sentiment galore
and falling face-flat, totally bedeviled
by the grandiosity of its plea
to weaken reality's hold
and give illusion its last final chance.

**BEING CAREFUL**

Life is our precious goal to preserve,
including avoiding a traffic accident
by watching the lights across the street
and not let your legs cross too soon
that motor-vehicle area as a pedestrian
with the smarts to be a safe public citizen.
A little care can assure a lot of future
if age has spared you some left.
Maintaining life with vigilance
includes all the health you can muster
including some life-sustaining exercise
including what help the doctors can provide
for which they've prepared with an expensive career
and studying a whole anatomy full of bones,
to which you'll be reduced when your weary flesh peels off
with a foot-bone left with which
to metaphorically as they say kick the bucket,
but you need a knee for that too,
not the one that your mourners will kneel on,
or two, pouring out pails of grief
from tear-splattered eyes. Don't forget
to have prepared your will in advance
as your friend, spare me some change if you will,
coins won't do, paper variety is the best
to add sums of arithmetic from the mess.

Death follows fast on the sturdy health
it systematically ruins, from corpse on down,
leaving what used to be you all bereft
just as consciousness abandons you, skull and all,
telephone number, even your name itself
that your loyal friends like me have known you by
and feel sorry that you had to precede them
into that amorphous residence that doesn't even exist.

## JANE AUSTEN'S CENSORED ENGLISH TRAGEDY

Your tale is sad? Here's another.
Jane Austen's six-daughters mother
schemed to marry, if not all, some
to local bachelors whose eligibility was won
by property-owning to an illegal sum;
and her daughters would realize a lifetime dream,
by marrying into this high-prized scheme.
But there was only one local eligible bachelor
(but really widower, as a matter of factueler).
So he had to marry all six of the daughters
which led to an unruly number of slaughters,
killing all but one of the six marauders;
but the mother died in the enterprise,
plus five of the daughters who lost their prize
in one fell swoop, in luck's random guise.
The surviving daughter clung to her husband
and learned at all odds to infinitely trust him.
Any household squabble, she'd bust him.
He succumbed to her threat, and knuckled under,
in their lightning life together, amidst thunder.
She'd gnaw on him with rapacious plunder
to eat away all organs his life would encumber,
a downfall to which he was chief succumber.
Sad tale of daughters originally six in number
(a tale for history to mercifully smother)

reduced to one, plus the dead mother
who started this whole business with a scheme
that would realize success in a six-fold dream
of innocent daughters of a large family
whose end was hardly a peace treaty of amity.

## ASKING FOR TOO MUCH? I HOPE NOT

Let's restore order in the world,
that has erupted with chaos unfurled.
Let's purr serenely like a cat curled
on the softest sofa or couch.
Too many creatures today are saying "ouch!"
while stealing money for inside their pouch.
Let havoc and murder subside.
Let scared people venture outside
and feel bold enough not to hide
from horrible terrors that await them
at the sign of somebody just humming "ahem."
Don't jump if you assign malice to "them."
It's just your imagination,
from whose hauntings take vacation
within the precincts of our nation
that mirrors the world at large.
If you spot an "enemy," you don't have to charge:
He may be a friend that you mistakenly dodge.
So what I appeal for is peace,
whose next step is to promote ease.
Don't get scared at the jump of a sneeze.
Harmony is what I advocate.
Be my buddy, be my mate.
Kick the teeth out from the monster of hate.

May malicious strife finally abate
and a boy ask a girl for a harmless date.
And if discord knocks, just let it wait.
Embrace the peace we urge to be our fate.

## SOME RUDE COUNSEL

Watch out what you expect.
What the imagination has pecked
from outer reality is bedecked
with an ultimate surprise,
like sunset instead of sunrise,
quite opposite your surmise.
So if you're shocked by the incident,
don't let your composure suffer an ugly dent
and hamper your future judgment.
Reality comes here. But then it went.
Think sequentially. Don't get bent.
Keep your anxiety fully pent:
Don't betray the whiff of its unseemly scent.
Advice on how to figure things out
comes at no expense, you lout.

## TIME'S PERMISSION TO BE LIVE ONCE

What a lousy deal that people have to die.
It's enough to make their survivors cry
but they too will be mourned one day
in their sad turn; turn and turn about.
Thus generations for the human race
mirror slower or swifter generations for other species
in the game time plays with creatures' lifetimes,
life being alive; and with death nothing happens,
an accumulation of nothing but nothings
in the vacuum emptied out of what once
happened characteristically to that one kind of life.
People are like insects or flowers.
Reproduction is fine for the future,
but succession of lives
leaves lots of room for the father types to die
and mothers—those noble carriers of the young.
You have to hit time at the right time
to have your time of being alive.
Good luck. The journey is long
or short, but very vivid
to the bland familiarity of yourself.

## AL, GONE

Al, I knew you so well. We were friends.
Then of our two inevitable ends,
yours happened first. So I was left to mourn.
We were both born
as contemporaries to be in the same class
in high school by geographic luck
and so we both came to pass
from out of school to the employment world
to find our lives and our wives too.
Meanwhile our friendship grew and grew.
And grew some more but ended unevenly,
you in death and me still stuck here
grateful for my time left, even without you
whose goodness to me is my only tribute I have left
in the pure memory game.

## INTERSPECIES MUTUAL SAFETY

Birds do me a favor,
when they come at me, to veer away.
Actually, it's for their own survival,
because I'm a solid object
that at their peril, they'd better avoid.
So don't credit them for saintly benevolence
that spares me awful discomfort
by collision: they're in the same boat
so to speak. That's a fishy compliment,
but they and I benefit
by jointly going collision-free.
I could kiss them for that
but risk getting pecked
even if my lips raided the target
with acrobat-like accuracy
at mid-wing
virtually at the peak of their beak
in the frenzy of their pique.

# I PLACE THE BIRDS ON A LOFTY PEDESTAL

The birds fly around the sky like they own it;
or did they steal it, as if from aborigines?
Uninterfered with, it's their free land,
map-free, diving in and out
by migratory patterns or improvisations
as food temptations slant across
their instinctive capturings.
From earlier pedigrees, long hail
these loose-limbed poetic symbols,
light as the wind, the easy goers
that need all their strength to survive.

# REMINISCENCES FROM A NEARLY DRAINED UP GLASS

What happened to my life?
Virtually all disappeared, save for memory.
Memory feeds my remaining years
plus vitamin supplements of
the here and now, the immediate,
the thrills of consciousness in action,
feebly matching the swashbuckling
of my more glamorous past
that memory proudly embroiders
or shyly signs off with modesty.

## SUBWAY PORNOGRAPHY

Looking across the subway aisle
while the train keeps zooming, you've got to file
that woman opposite, whose legs
shuffle their summer dress, which begs
admiration, though hardly from afar.
Then standing fat men block my vision, to jar
my presumed lustful ogling
of exquisite legs too mind-boggling
to ignore, even surreptitiously,
but I tried to look unsuspiciously,
waiting for the fat men to uncloud
my silent vision that was too loud
in this speeding subway car
with the gazed-on legs slightly ajar
and my furtive peeking
at where the ass met the thighs seeking.

# BETTER LINKED FOR KEEPING APART

When a bird avoids to collide with me
he's doing us both a great big favor.
He steers clear just in time
to convert an interspecies type of crime
to a stealth-swift-act of mutual benevolence
by acrobatic dodging, practically in mid-air,
and keeping us unacquainted strangers
rather than to incur perverse kinds of dangers
in violent terminal friendship
intimately unwise, the wrong connection.
There's wisdom in keeping your distance,
as people and birds, for instance.
They don't get too familiar.
Good neighbors mend separate fences
in the commonality of their defenses.

## TIME'S INFIDELITY TO ITSELF

Watch out. The world can fool you
by upsetting your predictions
so you have to re-adjust the mind
and try evaluation anew
on the contrary evidence from before.
The update from the latest experience
should be your new guidepost.
Rearranged expectations
turn askew the old world's order
and map the land with a new border.
Surprise? I'm used to it by now.
The bull is unfaithful to his former favorite cow.

## ASPECTS OF OUR KIND

Humans, that's what we are,
no other way we could have been born
granted what ancestry we had
and the chemical mixtures
in our joint makeup
and the defining characteristics
with variations on personalities
and the conditional luck factors
along the money route
and what happened to have happened
that later drove the circumstances.
Culture and gender play their parts too,
so what else is new?
Give me examples, for instance.
Well, the generalities pile up
and the specifics are too numerous.
People tell their stories
and look for the listeners.
The listeners and the tellers
are what we principally are.

## SOME MARRIAGES STAY

Is love life a fickle series
of "sworn love forever" followed by
"farewell, it's all over"?
If you live long enough, yes.
Unless marriage halts the sequence
so that the present gets prolonged
into permanent sincerity.
Marriage doesn't just sanctify
like an institution of enforced obedience
to its own rules and codes,
if, for once, sincerity
takes on a marathon role
and stops the sprinting novelty craze
of passion restoked at its battery
to phantomize an increasingly obscure past
into defaced signposts
along the aging way.
Hypocrisies were like torn pages
from the calendar's beating heart.
Circumstances intervened
when happenstance got serious
and ruled the past out.

## PROVISIONAL QUESTIONS

So is love forever?
But forever has a time limit
depending on—sometimes tragic—circumstances.
So forever is qualified
and drags its quantity clause
into any romance
even seasoned by passion
into a riot of necessity.
Love pleads inevitability,
even summoning the desperation excuse
at the pitch of urgency
with romance at its unbeatable heart.
As for irresistibility, that depends.
Other factors enter in.
No automatic guarantee
dipped in vapid certitude
dulls life's enterprising suspense.
What's going to happen next?
Whimsical chance opens a future door
with a hidden key.
"Hearts twist in the wind,"
dallying over a delayed outcome.

# EVEN IF YOU PERSONALLY DON'T CONTRIBUTE, YOU'RE BOUND TO BE A BENEFICIARY OF EVOLUTION, WITH ENOUGH LARGESS TO SUPPORT US ALL

1.

Our active procreation of evolution
is a collective masterpiece.
There's so much of us, it's bound to work
even though some participants shirk
in the fertility rating; we get it through
thanks to the rampant sexual passion
that nature endowed us according to our fashion.
We invest in posterity, and cash in.

2.

Evolution keeps the human race alive
so that it may collectively thrive
despite a few non-contributors
who certainly are not evolution's inhibitors.
We're in the overwhelming numerical majority
(even with our inferior seniority)
that affords to carry on our backs the non-contribution
of some people of weak sperms and vaginas
who beg off and don't add themselves
to babies who are already stored plentifully on the shelves,

because there's no shortage of the digs and delves
even though we don't do it ourselves.
Others do the lurching and plunging,
and we're the parasites in their crunching,
enjoying all of evolution's welfare.
With so much population, there's plenty to spare.
So let's collectively rejoice. It's all our share.

## A WORD BOND FRAYED. (IT'S TRUE, I'M AFRAID)

Oh multi-embodied world
of trees, cars, animals, people,
you world painted good and bad
by historians along the way,
the correspondents who break the news
and criticize morally:
I'll fill you in with the latest
from a humble shallow viewpoint:
I'm soon dying, and my participation
is poised between remembrance and nothing.
Even in spectatorship's passivity
I'm surely evaporating, there'll be no me
while your rental space, dear world,
welcomes the still-paying residents.
You have a different flavor in your breath
now that my inhalations grow weaker
and my lung supply refuses
to do my share in the earth's ozone
by the stratospheric standards
of health's inclusion
in our cooperative cycles.
By our energy exchange
I'm not measuring up to the resources
of your forwarding momentum.
Whom am I addressing?

Are you the earth or the world,
in your outsidedness?
Between us, a word bond
is barely all that's left
now that my actions turn introspective.
The auditory murmurings
attending my birth
now look to a deaf slate.
My portions of the pie
leave undistinguished
the edible and the crust.

## SORRY, READERSHIP

The tampering translator
changed the sex of the main character
in virtual novel-rape
causing a law suit
by publisher and author
which the translator avoided
through ... oh, spare the details
on this convoluted case
on linguistic literary mayhem
and gender-taking liberty.
It was a counter-creative crime
of reality presuming on fiction
in blatant interference
by a form of malicious theft
to puzzle the legal experts
and put the principals at odds:
publisher, translator, author,
and the character of molested gender.
How was this case decided? Don't ask.
I'm inadequate to this stupendous task.

## WHAT IS LIFE FROM THE INSIDE?

Life? I don't know what it is.
But I sure couldn't do without it.
That's more important than mere knowledge,
which is academic, abstract, beside the point.
To be practical, living life
is the real essence. It's at the heart of the matter.
It even describes itself
by first-hand knowledge.
Yes, the brain is an important component.
Let's not separate it
from life's full-fleshed quintessence.
Surely life is a brainy matter
in addition to what it really is—
which my brain doesn't really know.
How to reconcile this …
dichotomy?: Of life lived from the inside
and the knowledge that covers it all up
with missing the point?
What point? Don't go that far.

## KEEPING THINGS GOING

With lucky sperm that's ejaculated,
our generation has now created
the future's new young people
to worship in religion's steeple
and extend humanity's utmost grasp
into a further collective lustful gasp
while sacrificially we die out
thinning into skeletons while babies thrive stout.
Our turn is used up. That's why we pout.
We lose the game while begetting winners, no doubt.
So take it all in good grace
in keeping up evolution's slow but frenetic pace
landing somewhere in earth's outer space.

# THE BIRD ASSAULT

The birds fly around the sky like they own it,
infinite property rights way out of orbit,
and they have the mobility to keep mobile quite a bit,
and when they fly at me it gives me a fit,
and if I'm the target, I hope they miss it,
otherwise the garish lights of anxiety will be lit
to crush me as I depart forces with my wit,
and the threads of my sanity will be loosely knit,
and directly in my pathway, the birds don't merely sit,
to belt me into imbalance as I'm hit.
While being knocked down, I see the birds scatter and quit,
while I rest achingly in my improvised pit.
The serene birds mock their wings at me
and migrate softly over a distant sea.

# WHAT WE ALWAYS HAVE, UNLESS DEMENTIA COMES

Oh I remember this, I remember that,
all different types and colors,
all locked into my only brain
that divides them all into different era spans,
flirting with forgetfulness,
semi-oblivion, fading away;
popping up again, brand new
but altered, distorted, in a way,
having more to do with now than then.
Some are more important than others,
the forerunners of my current plans.
They're of different values and qualities,
ancient history dimmed,
or currencies, recent,
backed up into virtually now,
dealing with determined desires
and decisions smacked with impact
for my personal welfare.
Hello, you new arrivals,
jump aboard, help me.
You're welcome, till I forget you.
My needs always beget you
or needless coincidences
offhand, just tossed up with the pack.

Sometimes you haunt me, attack.
Or thanks just for reminding me
whether idle or necessary.
Some I value, some I bury.
You various bunch, I treat you unevenly.
When my body stops, you'll die along with me.

# THE EMOTIONAL LIFE, FULL OF FEELING

1.

I wish my brain would leave me alone
and behave its own true and lonely self
so I can neatly put my troubles on a shelf
where they can undergo a "forgotten" stage
in their ever moving livelihoods
browsing through a variety of moods
till the right ones stir alive again
and return my friendship with theirs again
to make good feelings replace the painful ones
and feeling "well" is simply a good deed
that lays down the law of how to succeed.

2.

A whole flock of good feelings I can breed
just by the simple and happy wish,
moving the brush or broom with a hefty swish.
That does the trick. Is it magic?
Whatever, steer clear of the tragic,
It's too contaminating
to be restful or accommodating.
Give yourself, finally, a restful break.

3.

How to manipulate your moods:
Cast out those annoying bad feelings
and cleverly reconfigure your dealings.
Breathe a frank load of wholesome breath
and escort doleful woes to a necessary death
and put misery out of its own misery,
restore life to its sweet mystery
without going into hysterics.
If too troubled, seek the medics,
who are paid to put paid
to the passing distress parade.

4.

Feelings and emotions. Take your pick.
Both can do the trick
of keeping us much too alive
to simply live and thrive.

# THE MYSTIQUE OF RELATIONSHIPS

1.

The more she loved me, the more I loved her back.
Sometimes it doesn't work that way between couples:
The more she loved me, the more indifferent I became.
The ways of chemistry are magically labyrinthine
and diversified into unique situations
instead of classified as a general rule.
The broken rule is the norm,
the rule of the broken thumb
that makes all analysis deaf and dumb
and blocks the skull into a lockjaw jam
hardly knowing who she is and what I am.
I once loved her. I tell her to scram.

2.

So scrambled was our relationship,
we rented it out to the movies
and even hired a built-in critic
unknown whether to praise or pan.
That's like controlling the medium, don't you think?
A contract drawn on invisible ink
and paper that melts to the touch.
The throat swallows uncontrollably into a clutch
believing too little and knowing too much.

# TO BE HAPPY, GET MISERABLE FIRST

Wanna be happy? Of course. Everybody does.
First get yourself anxious with a negative buzz.
Worry yourself almost to death.
Die before you run out of breath.
Then, it's my firm belief,
it's time to get relief.
Alleviate your state
and put yourself on a new slate.
Suddenly you realize, "What's there to be anxious about?
I'm so happy now. I'll arrange a shout
of sheer joy because the pressure is off.
I'm free. I'll pick my nose and then I'll cough.
Oh am I a new man now!
The bull has his way with the placid cow.
The man is hurt. Then he says 'ow!'
Then find out what change will allow.
And go there. Pursue your own glee;
and when you pay the bill, collect the fee.
If you want to feel better, you got to rebound.
From the tune of misery, you've got a better sound.
From falling off, you're on steady ground."

## COMPARING THE PAIR

Darwin only formulated it.
Evolution had preceded him by a million years
all by itself, gradually.
Then Darwin put his finger on it.
In Edison's case,
he invented the whole procedure
of electricity as a means of light.
One shed light, the other made it.
Both were okay. Neither will fade
from history's own hit parade.

## EVOLUTION DOESN'T NEED MY PRAISE, BUT HERE GOES

As for evolution, leave it to others,
who'll take up the slack if we don't contribute
with our lustful but barren efforts.
There's safety in numbers, so evolution will thrive
to concoct future generations and keep them alive
with enough sperm and ovulization
to fill the world with many a patriotic nation
and energy left over to make a wasteful war
which won't make a dent on evolution's robust core
which creates ancient history and much left in store
because there's no exhaustion for evolution,
its numerically powerful thrust is the solution
to world crises including pollution
and governmental corruption
and earthquake's occasioned eruption
that damns and shadows the surface
of the well-flawed earth, which does us service.

## THERE'S VIRTUALLY ENOUGH TIME FOR ANYTHING, ALMOST

Life is tumultuous to a serious degree
sometimes. As to other times, we'll see.
Time spaces all our feelings out
so that there's time for each to yell and shout:
"It's my turn. Give way."
Even depression has its day.
And now it's merriment's time to sing,
and now we'll see what the next moment will bring
as the years pile up
and the old dog was once a pup
having lived so many moods through
that changeability is the main clue
as to what ultimately itched him with a tick.
The old dog is up again to a new trick.
Even a leash can barely contain him
pursuing this, that, and every whim.
The moody dog has a lengthy life.
Every human's dog's-day is full of strife
piercely shrilled on our boisterous fife.
The gist of these hints—what's clear?
Combine your feelings, or divide them,
it sure adds up. So have good cheer;
and when emotions come, hide them
unless they burst their way through
and teach us what you can't or can do.

## ALLOTMENT OF CREDIT: ENGLAND'S REWARD

Did Darwin create evolution?
No, he only discovered it.
Give him credit, anyway,
for formulating how evolution keeps itself going
on its own accord, nice and easy,
on good old DNA,
which Darwin didn't even know about,
though admittedly history gave him clout
to give the whole ordeal out.
That's what his famous reputation
does for the whole English nation:
to get credit for all the credit he's been given,
down to the least scientific civilian.

## PASSABLY EASIER

I tried to write a passable poem,
but trying too hard, I only got stuck.
Then I resorted for divine guidance
from that marvelous man of myth, god,
but he was proven to not even exist.
Determined, I asked a muse for inspiration,
but she declared, "I'm only faintly amused."
So then I asked for self-help guidance
from a Buddhist guru from India
but scandal had proved him a quack.
Then I opened a poetry-writing manual
but that was underwritten, only for amateurs,
for which I was overqualified.
So then, in bitterness, I only wrote this,
which you can readily read above.
(Meanwhile, within my self-sufficient body,
urine had built up, so soon I'll take a piss
which comes out easily, unlike my difficult poem.)

## THE CONFUSION THAT BLENDS IN AT THE RIGHT TIME

Love's a mysterious entity
that signifies the end of me
or else the beginning in such rebirth
that the world is crushed into a new earth
that grows flowers in the sea
and rams the soil with fertile insects
at the point where astrology becomes astronomy
and knowledge gets polluted by myth
and corruption is at the intersect
between easy to believe and strongly suspect.
With a detective's lens, I stoop to inspect
the clues there are to solve a crime
that hasn't really begun in all of time,
to arrive so confused that the past is made up
to fill an abbreviated gap
between dangling on or crawling off the map.
As a wise man, I'm justly termed a sap.

## WHAT TO DO, JUST IN CASE

If life confuses you, you know what to do:
try a new tack. Instead of retreating, attack.
Convert off-white to a violent black
and substitute a dog's bark for a cow's usual moo.
If you follow my advice, I guarantee
that by multiplying "four" five times, you'll get "three."
If this doesn't make sense, then try to change
a narrow focus to a widening range
and formulaic orthodoxy to the novelty of the strange
and suspense into dull routine
and illusion's purple into nature's green
and immense surprise into quiet serene.
Wipe the slate abnormally clean
and you'll find that such a new you
will finally but not inescapably ensue.

# THE PRIVILEGED WOMAN WHO STILL WORRIES

This riot moon drives me so bizarre,
it's enough to put on backwards my brassiere.
Socially, have I made enough friends
without beseeching and seeking to make amends?
Is my health perked up by regular doctor visits,
or do I need remedies for the what-is-its?
Does my husband love me faithfully
and doesn't lie for coming home latefully?
Should soon a baby I should give birth to,
so I stop me-obsessing and go "goo-goo"?
Oh my nervous life! Please settle true.

# MARRIAGE CYCLE (in 4 parts)

1. TO MY WIFE, IN ACRID SWEETNESS

Occasional flareups will be dampened and subdued
between me and my lady love.
Nature gave to us on earth
what the birds easily have above.
My heart pours out such assistance
as her physical troubles demand
that my whole being is the physician
to keep my bird flying on the land.
Between us, our pulses flicker and stand.

2. MY WIFE, IN ALL HER YEARS

The tears I occasionally let descend
all in my wife's behalf
are for her troubles in eyes and lungs.
She's glad to have me there.
I pour out mercy from my heart
that has no medical talent.
Compassion lightens out of my eyes;
and so, to paraphrase along with Yeats,
and modern-eyes his tune,
I louder sing, the more tatters in her mortal dress.

## 3. I HELP MYSELF TO WHAT THE WORLD CAN GIVE

If my wife, who's occasionally tart,
distills her sweetness to the world,
only a few friends and relatives respond.
And so do I, as long as my might
derives energy from the world's hidden love
that bursts out, blazes above.

## 4. WE BICKER. OKAY, BUT SO WHAT?

Is love intangible?
Of course. But symbolized by real things.
So that can barely suggest
that I love, but not in jest,
my actual true-life love
called by marriage my wife,
as sociology or society unites
the two of us into proverbially one
despite occasional disputes.
Though we argue like brutes,
our beings couple and click wings.
Love is composed of such real things.
I flutter my heart-wrapped song
to my wife who quite kisses me along
and lectures me on what's wrong.

# THE LONG, NEEDY PROCESS AND ITS SURPRISINGLY ABRUPT END

You face the vacuum of nothing.
Fill it up with something.
But be fussy too: Not just with anything.
Make it count. Give it some heft.
Pour it in, but have something left.
Something for a rainy day
or to strike while the iron is hot
and sing to the shining of the sun
in those arching rhythms between work and fun.
But I need help: Someone?
So I went out and grabbed myself a wife.
Cute as a fiddle. Neat along the middle.
Curves in all the right places
and cosmetic makeup for her faces.
She fills the vacuum, which she displaces
with being the sweetheart of my heart
that you can't just buy in any mart.
Living with her is the finest art
that brings me up with a sudden start
that how lucky I surely was
to fit the sorely needed wife
to the vacuum she was made for
without knowing it, all her life.
But divorce ended our messy strife.

## HOW TO TAKE OR NOT TAKE THAT MYSTERY CALLED "LIFE"

This Life is full of fraught.
Solving anxiety results in naught.
Wasn't there a better Life I could have bought?
Or a better pair of genetic genes
to wipe my slate the better clean?
No, let's just take it as it comes,
Life's imperfections beat their own drums,
despite ennui, boredom, and the ho-hums
mingled with worry's fitful depression
and manic yelling out
of the spleen's burstful bout
that lets out our ugly vomit.
But yet, Life has a side that's comic.
It flashes in the meteor of the comet,
so let's all to Life commit
instead of succumb to a suicidal fit
and give in to wasteful despair
that drizzles our eyes with many a tear.

## PHILOSOPHY'S BEARING ON LIFE ITSELF, BY WAY OF INSIDE STRATEGY

Life has a philosophical dimension
which appropriately I ought to mention.
It gives us, but also relieves, tension.
When you consider what life is all about,
never leave the question of philosophy out.
Philosophy answers every problem you wish to ask
and creates a "knowledge atmosphere" in which to bask.
To relieve your mental insufficiency,
ignoring philosophy is a profound deficiency
in the art of understanding what life is all about.
Philosophy will whisper the answer, and shout.
Life may be inward, but its solution is out.

## LET THE GOING THING GO ON

The magnetic chasm between a man and a woman
contributes to evolution of the species
by the fundamental process all must obey
or else the human race dissolves in decay
and future babies neglect to be born, come what may.
Don't waste the potential of the sexual mechanism
to empower the force behind new generations
and never allow reproduction to take a vacation
from reinforcing our brilliant own human race
that now invents ways of invading outer space
in chemical compounding and physical prowess:
metals, plastic, and ingenuity
that keep the whole global planet up to its own beauty
by the process of its own velocity
under the dual ownership of sexual reciprocity.

## A LITERARY METAPHOR FOR SEXUAL NON-FULFILLINGNESS

I'm too old to satisfy a woman sexually,
like a book that misspells itself textually
with so many errors of grammar and syntax
that the book contains much less than it lacks
and imagines itself rather than adheres to facts.
This virtually non-existing book
literally from all libraries took
itself out of circulation
so that it can spare the nation
eye-strain and content-indigestion
that refuses to answer the question
of a book's validity
for those who wish to avoid stupidity.

## ANTI-THEATRICS

I love my wife. Is that a crime
against aesthetic dramatics, which craves new surprise
and suspenseful intrigue? How bourgeois
to keep on the same old track,
like going back again to a reel of going back.
As a dramatist, I'd be laughed off the stage
and put into an antiseptic cage
drama-free, with isolated boredom
to create an epidemic yawn
to collapse the public into a non-dawn
from which awakening would be difficult
but perhaps start a dullness cult
as a fresh perk for the avant-garde
and set the theater back to a deep retard.

# A TRIO OF OUR LOVE

## 1. HOW LONG WILL THE WELD WORK?

Two people together. Isn't that the deal?
Between them, the world bursts apart
and returns in a totally different shape
wherein the combinations wed them
as crucially their worlds unite
with problems in the intermingling
soluble once the spat is over
and love throws its big blue bruise
over them for a doubly lonely cruise
down two rivers from the same water
along the hedges, and down the border.
Two former beings plunged in a new order.

## 2. TOGETHER BY TUNES OF TINY TURNS

Loving her is so easy I breeze through it.
Looking is one way and hearing is another
when she listens to me as I brush over her
and what we tell one another is important
in an adventure so mutual our memories are there
to record the same episode from views so converging
that giving and taking come in the same business deal
and I take her part, and she takes mine
exchanging our empathies
into the envelopment that's both of us.

## 3. US, NO LESS

A love duet. That's all you get.
But first we have to have met.
At least that much, to clinch the bet.
Each in each other's debt.
The rooms were vacant. Now they're let.
The order is up: a total set.

# THE LIFE SCIENCE DEPARTMENT'S INADEQUATE PSEUDO BIOLOGY'S FRAUDULENT PROFESSOR IS SUPPOSED TO TEACH DARWIN

Darwin's such a great celebrity,
the ages thunder his applause.
But who ever dreamed of reading
his too technical scientific book?
I did. So celebrate me. Through hook or crook
I read it through—but only by skimming.
Otherwise, it's too like swimming
with a dull bronze iron weight against the waves.
But history has accorded him numerous raves.
So we celebrate *Descent of the Species*,
despite it's never ever so easies
to grasp what he's talking about
which earned him his universal clout;
so I looked into the book, and out.
I passed my earnest scholarship
by entering his book, for a little dip
like tasting his brew, but just a bare sip
in professorial Darwinianship
to claim authenticated credentials
and earn all the academic essentials
to avoid the penitentials
of collegiate exposure as a fraud.
Don't whisper a breath of this abroad.

I have a wife and three kids to support.
If only I'm sacked, my whole career comes to naught
and family poverty, if I'm caught.
Disgrace will become my final report,
and "species extinction," as Darwin says,
using his own prophetic phrase
to put terminus to my cheating ways
and end the promise of my student days.

# A LOFTY, YET EARTHLY, COMPARISON

The squirrel knows how to keep itself alive.
So does that sky-denizen, the bird, know to thrive
by feeding on sundry leftovers here and there
to fill its diet requirements to a minimum bare.
The squirrel is almost a bird the way it can climb
with trees available for its body to rhyme
with fetching branches tending upward.
Though handicapped by no wings, still it could
virtually almost match the bird on high
with its proclivity to outdo the sky.
Is there a moral discernible in this?
Sure. When compiling enough urine, it's time to piss.
Can a squirrel's soaring catch the bird's?
Not till your eating changes to turds.

## A PERSONAL PLEA TO THE PRESS

Numerous subjects abound to write about.
Probe them all, and give me a shout.
Even the major worthiest let us know,
don't just let the wind take it and blow.
But hasn't already everything been said
(like who of all people is in whose bed)
from primal gossip and the rumor mill?
So whatever your findings, give it a spill.
Let the human entertainment have a maw-full
of superior news of the category "awful."
As a newspaper reporter, your fee will be high
to raise the reader's envy and indignant cry
that the world is spinning toward the unfair
and the readers' chorus raises the tone of despair
from what comes out from underground into the very air
how the wind will harshly blow
but us citizens have a right to know.

## THE WAITER SAVES THE DAY

When stuck in melancholic halls of brooding,
I seek consolation at a restaurant for fooding
where the customer and the waiter are colluding.
"Waiter, what food will make me feel all right?"
"What enters your mouth, sir, then takes flight
into your inner stomach and private bowels
to change your gloomy moods into restorative bestowals."
I heed his advice, and now I feel fine,
think of giving a large tip, but that's too benign.

## THE HENCE & THE WHENCE

Love is a factor in human life.
Hence every husband has a wife.
Also, she has him, of course,
though they argue who's boss.
Maybe she's more equal than he.
But they both descended from the upper tree,
their ancestors being apes.
My mind reels and gapes.
How did this all come to be?
We're tightly wound
but boundless free
so ape may come down
from his lofty pedigree
and turn into us right here:
crazy owners of this sphere
that spreads along the near and dear
with rivers that break up the earth
as viewed from an airplane berth.

# EVOLUTION INTRIGUES

1. IT'S BEYOND ME

Life, of course, is quite a puzzle.
About it, I can speak, not muzzle
my ideas about what it's like
to whiz down the turnpike
of life in its full span
from born baby to mortal man.
But my mental apparatus can't scan
the mystery, and how it began,
by a mere conscious effort.
Retreating from the challenge, I exit
from the physical strain involved
of wondering how I evolved.

2. THE LONG VIEW, ULTIMATELY SAD

Nature seems to separate men and women
for the sake of evolutionary reproduction.
Men produce the required semen
and women the receptacle vehicle
which biology has donated to evolution
in favor of advancing the ambitious project
of DNA's sure mechanical survival
as an immense factor for the human race
to roll along uninterrupted

by time; but time instead is recruited
to slow down or speed up
history's push ahead, to where?
To despair along the way, and death—
a permanent stoppage of breath.
So evolution tolls up its victims:
martyrs to the killjoy of mortality.

# PRESERVING RETAINED FADING MEMORY BLOSSOMS

When a friendship ends badly, with a misunderstanding or spat or spite or accusations or bitterness or insults or sour grapes; or just simple indifference, no matter who rejected the other, or by mutual letting go: Don't discount those memories of when that friendship indeed flourished. The moments when you were truly friends shouldn't fall victim to the phasing out, indifference, anti-climaxes, or whatever dissolution of a valuable period of your life: For what is more valuable than moments of harmony and love in a human relationship? You needn't judge your relationship memories by a strict structural formula of beginning, middle, and end, like a play, novel, or film. Those precious moments of life—when magic between friends or lovers was active: Don't deprive your dearest recollection scrapbook treasury in later times—a private reappreciation festival—leading to lonely old age and forgetfulness doom.

# **PUBLICATION'S FAILURE PROJECT**

What does a writer require of publishers?
Publication. What does he further require?
Publicity. What is his circulatory requirement?
Public libraries. What is his ultimate requirement?
Public fame. What's the consolation for missing it?
The pub, for guzzling or sipping
public liquid either strong or insipid,
to hurry down or just dip itself in.
Where ends his required publication?
The grave (make no bones about it)
where publication is not an entry visa.

# CONTEMPLATING THE QUINTESSENTIAL ESSENCE

What is the essence of life?
It must include a lot of strife
between you and yourself, and you and others,
you all come from a load of mothers,
as rivals and competitors for life's dearest breathing space,
hence incessant conflicts, not always with grace.
So life is full of offense and defense
fraught with struggle. Contemplating "whence?"
is a luxury. Survival can be brutal.
For some indeed, it's just too futile.
Not all conditions are bound to suit all.
It's not songs and dances from the Music Hall.
With this heap of humanity, no wonder it's a brawl.
Despite ideal loftiness, there's a scrounching fall.
Who said that life was just a waltzy ball?

## THAT OLD TANTALIZING SEARCH

Is philosophical curiosity practical?
It flirts with the positively actual
but misses it by a foot or an inch.
Yet it's close enough, so don't flinch.
You can smell it almost, through your nasal pores.
It scrambles to the ceiling, or the floors
on which you kneel to look everywhere
to catch the philosophical without its clothing bare,
and narrowly reach to the places I wouldn't dare
to perch, only philosophy leads me on
to find a substance upon which to dwell upon,
even thus ungrammatically. I can't leave the course I'm on,
it gets so close, I'm in a hot wet fever
to become the right kind of a non-believer.
Or does my ambition find me a self-deceiver?

## POLITICALLY ANGRY

1.

This world seems never to be satisfactory,
the way it's set up
and plays out. Its leaders
don't always think of everyone
but give preferential treatment to the preferred some
(in the richer bracket)
at most other people's expense,
who then squawk and try to speak out
but lack the organized power to do so
and are oppressed by the leaders
who quietly keep them quiet
(upsetting the legal system)
by imposing unfair punishments
to keep them in their "place."

2.

Well, that's unjust.
The ones at the top
are given corruption opportunities
extremely hard to morally resist,
leading to wealth at others' expense,
leaving the downside ones to suffer
by the imposed deprivations.

Politically, this has been happening
and to a cruel measure, too,
world-wide.

3.

Well, what to do, in humanity's cause?
Try to get enough resisters in office
to enough extent to oppose the oppressors
and improve the "system"?
The system is rigged to keep the oppressed powerless
and fearful for the penalties incurred
by even mild, token resistance.
Prison punishment keeps the status quo
and the oppressed can't even minimally flourish.
Humanitarian crises ensue.
The unfairness becomes endemic.
The world is being blown up
in favor of the few heads
harsh enough to keep the lead
and lead the resisters
to metaphorically bleed, and sometimes
actually too
in too many cases
in an unfair world where the spoils
get unequally divided.

4.

Is this a poetic voice speaking by an activist?
No, a voice in a crowd
in the bottomless middle class
making noises for a protest
that causes the leaders to crush it
and double down on their cruelty,
giving "democracy" a sadistic flavor
to heighten the dramatic irony
the further to sweeten outrage's iron wheels.

## CURIOSITY GETS FATIGUED

Oh the world is such an interesting subject
that we're subject to a curiosity of what it's like.
Many descriptions of the world have come down
the pipeline from commentaries obscure and plain.
It's all an attempt to conjure and explain
what's going on in the big broad world.
Can we narrow it down to the simple oyster that's pearled?
Not enough information. What else has unfurled?
We can't find out all at once
what the world is all about. But I'm no dunce.
My strategy is to look it up.
There my concern ends, and I'll go and sup.
I sup-pose that'll end the question.
My ignorance is a solid concrete bastion.

## THE SAINT, ALMOST

Dazed by coffee potency,
I overreacted to the universe
by being ultra-sensitive
to its dynamic blazes of sense impressions
on its walking horde of humanity
of which I, punyly, numbered one:
taking on the full blast
of feelings received by everyone else
by over-identifying
in my compassionitis
with human nerve endings
along the switchboard of receptions and emissions
due to everyone's impact on each other
locally or from far away.
That was how I liked to play.
It suffered me pain and pleasure
on the interactive board of my leisure
and sympathy overload
by my internal code
for truly everyone of my species.
Of undertakings, it wasn't the easiest.
Did that candidate me as a saint?
If it did, I'm about to faint.
Is it bombast on my part
or just the dizzying path of my art

to assume a pretentious role
that was immodesty's goal?
I'll have to withdraw a little.
I'll collapse, I'm too brittle
and took on more than I can take.
Am I too genuine to be such a fake?
I've got to rein myself in
and dive and duck from too much spin
due to violent effects on my skin.
I've lost out. Is that a win?
My hallucinatory episode
turned into this ode.

## DEFENDING DARWIN'S FAME (BUT I'M NOT A LAWYER)

Sexual differentiation can be quite distinct.
It's his method of delineation, as inked:
Darwin blueprinted it that way,
predicting future DNA
to keep the human race running.
It was Evolution he was gunning
to keep going apace. What an ambition!
It's been brought to fruition.
Then all hail Darwin's mind.
He's the genesis of humankind,
via Evolution,
immune to pollution.
What?! He didn't invent it?
He merely sent it
as a discovery application
to a scientific foundation?
What an anti-climax!
I'll protest with a fax.
He still deserves appreciation
and generations-long admiration.
He did the footwork.
Let's our acknowledgment never shirk
that his fame is deserved
for all that he observed.

From his task he never swerved
and said that physics is curved.
No—that's Einstein's domain!
Don't make me have to explain.
It's a crooked task, not plain.

## CAPACITY

My skin houses me.
My apartment houses the skin that houses me.
The outside world houses the package of before.
The universe houses the outside world which, etc.
Containers outside containers.
Or from the other angle,
containers inside containers,
leading to the me inside my skin.
Where do we end, or begin?
The out is in to something else.
Finally, what is a self?
A small atom, or that which contains all?
Or is the size irrelevant
despite direction's kinetic energy?

## **KEEP UP OUR COLLECTIVE GOING ON**

Sex populates the world.
That's why it's so popular?
No, its popularity is owing to
how nice it feels, whether it results
in kids or not.
I kid you not.
So don't get sentimental
in saying how we sacrifice ourselves
for the sake of adding to the world
cute little babies and all that,
whole new generations, unfurled,
so that evolution will be unimpeded
and humanity will go undefeated
in its everlasting plodding success
in keeping instinct unextinct
and the whole race alive
to the melody of "We thrive."

## CREATING VIA ORIGINALITY

You feel the rhythms surge,
submit to any urge,
don't let the mood diverge
while the fit is on you.
Make everything link true
to the one central theme,
the work of a unified team
subservient to the dream
that cruises passionately
but not too fashionably
in your mental head of blood.
Take it at the extreme flood
and go on from there.
Discover its own where.

# THE WHOLE THING. WHAT IS IT?

Love, life, and nature all collude
so as not to intrude
on philosophical guessing
and metaphysical questing
of what's behind all this.
What's about this weird bliss
of living in the actual world?
All sweet and sour unfurled.
I don't know how
life appeared. But take a bow,
dear world. You're the rental agent
that allows us to smell the whole pageant.
From dusk to dawn and all the way,
the world's arena is where we play
but have to work it out
to compete in the strenuous bout
between what to do and when not.
The choices, unraveled from the tough knot.
There's yes and no and but.
The when, the where, the what.
The life I'm endowed with,
the reality as myth.
The distance, and the width.

## OUR UNIQUE TWO-WAY WORLD LANDLORD

The world is the largest rental agent
but millions of evictions are going on,
some too painful to mention,
but forced upon our attention
by the fascination of fatalities
numbing us to banalities
of commiseration and private weeping.
Death graduates from our sleeping.
Funeral homes and memorials
with stirring testimonials
attended by freeloaders unfamiliar to families
of the bereaved,
are what's weaved
in the mix of the partings and arrivals
in the busy transforming world
of terminal procedures unfurled
and the births of the unborn
to temper the misery of the forlorn.
Coming and going are the people.
The broom switches both ways in a sweep-le.
The world rents in and out, to the well and the feeble
with crazy traffic irregularities;
workers neglect to attend their stations
but the world triumphs over all agents
in giving people their home:
the ones vanished, and those free to roam.

## THOSE TWO ENDS OF THE UNIVERSE

The best and only place for birth
is our good old familiar earth.
But also in the mix, those who depart
are returned empty to their station, dumb or smart.
The graves receive the done-in ones
having brushed the tape with their indifferent runs,
reduced to a brittle smear of bones
attended by a funeral mob and their beleaguered groans
of pity for their own future selves
with their cleared-away transparent shelves
of material goods they once owned
before their seemly flesh got good and boned.
Please forgive, for these sentiments intoned.

# HOW INTELLECTUALLY TO TRANSCEND WHAT YOU DEPARTED FROM

The fertile center of the mind
is where the best ideas come from.
They storm from the vertex
(or is "vortex" the proper word?)
and drum up their context
surrounded by circumstance
to broaden out the situation
and lengthen its possibilities
whereby ideas fall into place
and solidify from the many to the few
by elimination's process
to surround something new
not thought of before
which will provide a leaping-out place
to displace the lazy old ideas
that leave themselves in the arrears
having usefully done their service.
Then I'll summon the words to serve it.
"It?" What's it?
Nothing less than the pith,
or even essence if you please,
of what I've come up with, with ease,
once the process has been exerted.
(Unless, of course, it's been perverted

by mistakes I'll never correct.)
PERFECTION don't you dare expect.
That's something you simply must reject
if you embark on any work at all,
reducing the larger gains to the minor small.
Does this seem like a paradoxical fuss?
Yes, to confuse and excite us.

# TWO JIMMY POEMS

## 1. TEARS FOR A FRIEND

Earth, receive a wept-over guest.
The great Jimmy Stagno is laid to rest.
I loved him in friendship's glory.
I'm still around, but I'm sorry
to report his miserable demise.
Only remembrance will suffice
that his life's lengthy lice-
ence terminates with me to mourn.
(To Jimmy: "Thank you for being born.")

## 2. MY ACCOMPLISHED FRIEND'S TOTAL LOSS

Poor Jimmy Stagno. Being dead
reverses him from being ahead
in the status championship of life.
He excelled others in wit's stiff strife
and in athletic competition.
He won trophies; and ambition
in sports was stifled only
by unlucky injuries. Otherwise, "if only"
he had escaped them, he'd be a champ.
At any event, his corpse is fresh and damp.
Thus, the best in wit and sports
loses all, and there are no retorts.

## IS A VERY OLD MAN'S ERECTION LIKE A STERILE STILL-BIRTH THAT PRODUCES NOT EVEN A BABY'S GHOST?

One by one, my friends suffer death.
Death prevents anything from happening next.
That's especially true in the matter of sex.
Before death, impotence is a prelude,
a rehearsal, even if you're nude.
Try an erection, don't be a prude.
But nothing comes out of it, I'm afraid,
even if the woman is only a maid
who's urging you on, but you can't let go
so your sex machinery is in a state of woe
while death impatiently walks to and fro
like a fretful father expecting a baby
which his wife can't deliver,
so her pregnancy bursts up its liver,
and it's a still-birth, like your vexed erection
"to" which it doesn't fruitfully have any direction
so it eats itself up, like a sterile nut,
unconditionally, there's not even a "but"
whether you live in a mansion or in a hut.
Then goodbye to life, with sex alongside
just to join in the merry ride
"to the other side."
But where is that?
Who knows? There's no doormat.

## LIFE AT ITS EXCESS POINTS, WHERE CORRELATIVES COME INTO PLAY, TO PRODUCE A SANITY-CONDUCIVE BLUEPRINT

Is life too emotional at times?
Not only that, it's passionate!
Is it a bundle of nerves?
However you slice it, that's the serve.
Its curve ball is known to swerve.
So the intellect comes to the rescue
just on the urgency of its cue.
Planning ahead, it concocts strategy
to anticipate what may lurk ahead
to meet possible disaster at its head
so you may earn your butter and bread
and parcel it out so neat and fine
that you approach life's majestic design
and instead of being torn apart, say "it's mine."
Design and all, life is me!
But don't work yourself up to a frenzy.
Take it as it is; can't you see?
Use your head, and also your body.
Treat them both as your buddy
to keep you straight in an emergency.
Homeostasis is your friend.
Don't go around the deep bend
where all bearings are lost

and insanity is your cost.
No, don't go crazy.
If you do, then amaze me:
Put on a show, at least,
and let out your inner beast,
that starves itself into a feast.

## THE EARLIER–LATER TESTS BY ONESELF ON ONESELF IN LIVING EXPERIENCE

Expectation is the comparison point with what later happens.

So in situations where it turned out that my expectations had proven, by unpleasant disappointment or embarrassment, to be excessive, I learned to modify expectation down lower, and become reconciled to this partial resignation.

Experience had become the re-adjuster. My expectations were now re-aligned with a new, more soberingly realistic "reality," a more successful sense of predictability.

Still, this resignation didn't always stick. Seemingly irrational "hope" would occasionally pop up again in my eternally renewing "heart," before it finally, soberly, died down, in that set of situations. My somberness lapsed to indifference, tempered by occasional daydreams or relapses of regret and loss. This being life, what can you expect?

## **WOMEN'S DISTINGUISHED LOSS**

If David Evers has died, where am I?
I'm down here, but he's not up in the sky
unlike some clerical people wish.
He's even below me, without a stitch
of amorous flesh on his romantic bones.
I hear the women sighing, with their moans,
his stiff erections missed by these new crones.

## IT'S EITHER ROUND THEY GO, OR NOTHING AT ALL

The leaves have gone missing "upstairs,"
but now if you'll redirect—down—all your stares
you'll find them all in a dead mess on the ground
while raking park attendants chase them around
if the wind stirs those elusive leaves
and the bereft summer woefully grieves
that autumn is now the new boss
transitioning to winter, while spring is at a loss
to find it—amazing—so far behind
in the calendar's circuitry, it strikes you blind
that all the seasons are in such a bind
to succeed each other in regularity
which none in the least rate any disparity.
They vie each other for utmost popularity.
Who's your favorite? I pick summer.
But none the rest is any bummer.
So treat the calendar with religious fastness,
Church to no season's lastness
in nature's zest of competition.
Each season's its own fruition.
None redound of superfluity.
For the efficacy of continuity,
I think all in a round they go,
but if their motion grates to a halt,

then life itself will find itself stalled
and your death will be piercingly announced
if the season's merry-go-round is trounced
and the machinery goes out of whack.
You can't have that perfect device back.
They all die at once. That's the lack.
The sky's then a permanent black.

## HOW TO LET ASTRONOMY PROTECT YOUR LAZINESS

Does the earth have a fixed orbit?
Sure it does. So absorb it
into your head to obey the rules
to use all the planetary tools
to keep the earth on a steady course
to maximize its powerful force
so that everybody on the planet alive
won't fall off, but instead thrive
by getting into the gravitational stride
(that without sweat you simply abide)
with a flexible thump of up and down.
Protect your arrears, so to keep your crown
in quite a universal balance
of upright posture. Doesn't that make sense?
No, you don't have to do a thing.
Astronomy is automatic: it won't take wing
and fly away to leave you alone.
Fool! You don't even have to lift a bone,
or try to spruce up your inner tone.
Let astronomy work for you. Be passive.
Just sit still, and keep your ass stiff.
Or soften up your flexibility
and obey evolution's fertility

that, while you're asleep, does all the work
and your duty is simply to shirk,
be idle, and enjoy your perk.
You've got it made. Don't juggle it, jerk.

# TWO VIEWS OF THE WORLD, INCLUDING SELF

1. RALLYING

The world is really scary, don't you think?
You can get hurt, before you even blink.
Peril dwells everywhere, so get scared.
The world is automatically nightmared
before you even go to sleep.
So you can begin now, to start your weep.
Your heart can't go anymore, but it's what you have to keep.
So go ahead, be afraid
and evil will make a late night raid
on all your reflexes, and shrink you down
to a shrivelly messy clown
that wears in reverse the world's absurd crown.
But don't let it get you down.
Get right up, and fight again
with your fists up now, don't ask when,
and cast yourself among the roles of men.

2. MIXED UP

The world is funny, ha ha ha.
Go crawling back and whining to your ma.
If it's so funny, why is it so sad?
Such ambiguity—it can make you mad.
Confusion reigns that way.

It not only reigns—it pours, so go away
and come back again another day
when safe to go out and simply play.
This regression to childhood
is against adult aggression on which we brood.
Time to go home now; refuge in food,
and contemplate on the world's remaining good
when on good behavior we children stood.

# I WIN BY A STONE'S THROW

The hard life of a stone
mocks mine, whose anatomical bone
is worn right through to the knob
with the drained blood that can still throb
from the rust-stained veins
that prop my whole pulse upright
to keep up my strenuous fight
to equal the hard life of a stone
whose stoicism emits no moan
nor the least intellectual groan.
More brittle than a stone,
but that's the life that I own
for better or worse.
Lack of money is my only curse
as I course through my life-through
under stormy skies or blue;
and of life's benefits, few
equal dullness status of a stone.
On that comparison, let me alone
to pursue my unstony life, ripe to the bone.
This comparison, in my favor,
lets me at life's rainbow of flavor
as opposed to a stonelike existence
that I'd never call life in an instance.
Of the two, I prefer my own stance:

which you could easily see, at a glance,
an obvious non-comparison
taking a rude optical chance.
If you call me a stone, it's in vain.
How capable I am of pain
shears us easily apart.
The stone's a dunce. I'm smart,
without even to belittle the point.
With me, life's in a better joint.
I'm the stone's appointed superior.
My image flashes best in a mirror,
more vivacious to a fault.
Much more lifelike, for all't.
I act the bully over a poor stone.
In all pity, let me let it alone.
The stone's my inferior?
Go ask yourself: "Who's superior?"
To my wife, I'm dearer.
She can vouch for me.
(But ouch! A stone can hit me.)
Her freedom of act
seals the whole pact.

# FARMING THE OBVIOUS, RISKING UNPOPULARITY THEREBY

1.

Stones are more substantial than clouds,
even when clouds get puffed full of rain.
This is a truth I can easily say aloud
without fear of inspiring disdain.
Stones are so hard, they're safely ignored
till you're quite indifferently bored.
So why needs a stone's hardness be said?
Because I have nothing else to say instead.

2.

A soft meditation on stones' hardness,
if you rake leaves, is like a yard's mess
when autumn falls from the trees
and inspires no buzz from the bees.

3.

The density of stones
exceeds human bones'.
"So what!" I proclaim.
"What's this obvious truism's aim?
There's no originality in this claim."

4.

A stone, through and through,
is tough as a nail all around.
Its density will truly abound
till your face riots in purple blue
at hearing remarks so dull
and drearily unhelpful,
unlike a more interesting thesis
on the celebrity Jesus
or "How to Conduct Your Life,"
whose vitalities are much more rife
than dreary meditations on a stone.
May my apology atone.

5.

Obvious truisms
should become few-isms
so as not to bore.
Of wisdom, that's my store
down to its dismal core.

## WHAT AT FIRST SEEMED LIKE DESPERATE ACTION TURNS UNNECESSARY

The world is coming to an end.
I'm going around the bend.
From whom our lives to fend?
The world is falling apart.
Suddenly, we must get smart
and do our frantic part
before we're ruined. Let's start.
No, I'm afraid it's too late.
The barbarians have plunged the gate
and toyed with our ultimate fate.
Or so the media has informed
gullible us. Was it a hoax?
That would be preferable, folks.
Comedians prankly make jokes
and we fall for them. It provokes
us to want to fight back.
Time for us to get off the fence
and take a stand some way.
Stand? Political you mean?
Then I must defend, or demean,
if we know what we're fighting before or against.
Time to get off the fence
and prepare the action we don't have to take
if only we knew how to bake what cake

and what are we doing being bakers
or have we been taken? Or are we takers?
No, we're achers:
Achers for love
and all the supreme things above.

## ADVICE TO CONSTANTLY TAKE

1.

Always improve what's bad
to a level far above the sad
and consequently you feel better
in the barometer of your mood setter.
Take my advice to the letter.
Make sure your past is always worse
than what you are currently. Now rehearse.
In other words, improve.
From a low skid, raise your groove.
That's the right direction to move,
so that your emotions from a zero
proclaim you their favorite hero
and tell you how to here go
from the worst up to the summit.
Your low state? Overcome it.
Impossible? No, now you've done it.
Your peace of mind? You won it.

2.

Alleviate all your woes
and overcome life's worst blows.
Feel better? It shows.
Rectify what's always bad

and eliminate the dismal sad.
Protect your comfort zone.
Improve it to your favorite own.
Then bad feelings will have flown
so the feat of having a good day
is your constant toy with which to play.
For finality, you've found the way.
When you've reached the pinnacle, stay.

## MOODS AND STOMACHS

Rehabilitate yourself with food.
If you're in a lousy mood
do yourself good and have a snack
to give that bad mood a good smack
and get a much better mood back
with a fuller stomach
making your old mood seem comic
by this act of therapy.
Fall asleep. Then get up to pee
and ask yourself, "How do I feel?"
Much better. I've made a good deal
by trading in my former bad mood
for a stomach ache with some lousy food.
But I won't vomit. So that's good,
having cured myself the best way I could.
The moral of this unofficial sermon
that I'm quite keenly firm on
to boost the mood that I squirm in,
is that taking a little snack
is to eat (despite faulty digestion)
as a restorative. Next question?
Ah. This is the mood I'm best in,
though my queasy stomach feels messed in.
Spiritually, I feel blessed in
the overall good I've derived from

the food and then the pill I've survived from.
Thus, I serve my body well
in which I'm doomed to dwell.
There's no knell yet of the bell
and no need to find a hotel
in the precincts of hell.

# TURN-TAKING: THE ART OF DISPLACING ME

1.

Love, kisses, and all that
derive from life's early stage
simply called youth
where romance is a real truth
and lust one of its sidekicks
to do with cunts and pricks.
Meanwhile, old age has been building
through intermediary stages
to turn the final pages
into sickly impotence.
Does that make any sense?
Yes, to kick me off the stage
with my baggage of old age
to make room for an earlier stage
of infantile pricks and cunts
(in an age of innocence)
that gradually looms larger
& becomes the barger-
in of their own prime
to live it up and have a good time;
while I, on the contrary,
become too dead to make merry.
That's turn-taking. Very.

2.

Now that I feel displaced
I'm made redundant. That's the case
to occur any old place.
I turn the other face
and am renewed by a baby.
Really? No, maybe.

## WHAT HAS ESCAPE RESCUED ME FROM, IF IT DID? AFTER HAVING UNDERGONE WHAT?

The wild passage through the psyche
psyches me out, that's the key
to letting your mind go to pieces
till it finally finds its eases
at the pressure point where it squeezes
through to a grand new idea
that liberates you from neurotic fear
for which the inner brain rises to a cheer.
But must you go crazy to do so,
like the operatic throat of Caruso,
intense with well-practiced discipline
so when he sits down it won't be on a pin
that points its sharp needle-like front
against the skin till blood comes out with a grunt?
No, not like that. So settle your mind
like in burlesque, the hips don't have to grind
your pelvis to pieces. No, what you find
is some form of exquisite peace
that lulls you into obituary's ease
through which your nostrils explode to a sneeze
and your legs buckle at the knee
and bones cry out, "Don't mess with me!"
I don't understand how then I can come to see
the puzzling end to an infernal mystery

that doesn't remotely touch on me.
What am I doing here? Let me get out
and find a new way I can shuffle about
without having to drown my agony in shout.
Taming yourself to calm down from psychosis.
you verged perilously on the closest
you ever came to the leastest mostest.
Barely emerging, yes, but from what?
All this bustle leads to an invisible dot.
If you have a pen, then compel it to blot.

## A SOCIAL COMPLAINT, THEN A PRIVATE DENIAL

Why is humanity
so given to profanity
that it all comes out in a curse?
And whom do we reimburse
for this commercial drivel
that sneaks beneath the civil?
We're bombarded right and left
with obscenity, of taste bereft,
and vulgarity strikingly crude
that nakedly implores the nude.
Aren't we ever fastidious?
Then you have to go on and pity us.
(But don't accuse me: I'm not a prude.)

## HISTORY'S SECRETED HUSH-HUSH ON THE WAY OVER

Columbus reserved his major energy for discovering America. During the voyage he used his minor energy to form homosexual relationships with assorted members of his crew, over whom, as captain, he had dominion. This exhausted him, so when America was finally reached, his crew boyfriends took his early place with the dark new natives whom gladly but dangerously they chanced upon. The crew reserved the more delectable of the natives for Columbus himself, to investigate intimately closely.

Luckily, Columbus' Spanish bosses, who bankrolled the journey, looked shyly the other way, breathing no breath of this to later historians, who anyway would have taken a vow of secrecy so as not to overshadow the main event's obviously significant priority. This informational discretion kept lips shut firmly intact till I have just spilled the beans.

My report has been neither verified nor confirmed, but no matter: it's too late to make a difference, because already America has made its dent on the new world, and its founder holds firmly to his eternal niche as if he had maintained chastity on the whole way over, & even beyond, however unnatural that would now seem in our overliberated times that gruesomely blare out its excesses with neither shame nor compunction.

## A MECHANICAL FAILURE

The train had a one-track mind
in his usual daily grind.
The track directed him where to go.
He was on the right track, to and fro.
That's what he was trained to be
or else he's completely at sea
when it comes to his occupation.
He can't just take a vacation
when passengers are impatient to get to work.
Now's the time for the train not to shirk.
Pressure drives him off the rails,
passengers get hurt, routine fails,
maybe a loosening of too many nails,
nuts and bolts in his constitution
made him lose his resolution.
If you want more, seek headlines
from local tabloids, in their own grinds.
Maybe you can read between the lines
and see what the tragedy underlines.

# THE MISPLACED WRITER IN A NEW ERA

Can I tame my imagination?
Don't treat it like a wild animal
to be harnessed as in a zoo.
Let it supply innovations
to what already seems to be true
but needs ready attachments
to enhancements that Form will do
in building the whole thing up
as a new entity all by itself
and add new pages to books on the shelf
to give kindly to an indifferent world
already preoccupied with alien things now
so that I'm left to fret by myself
with silly hopings for a smidgen of fame
in the uphill struggle with the writing game.

# A SELF-DESCRIPTION

Confusion reigns, so I try to cope
with whatever's within my scope
within the precincts of hope;
with situations and predicaments,
not to mention circumstances
and for other instances
that new contexts will dictate
upon which I fixate
all alertness pixelated
so I can be well adjusted
to whatever happens to pop up
and lands in my eye-ful cup
or hits upon my listening ear
with messages of doom or cheer
from reality's outer world
that the incoming wind has swirled
to introduce to consciousness
that reigns inside my head
where officially I reside
to learn what to decide
in case of emergency
and its consequent urgency
for which I'll be resourceful
to prevent anything awful
on my personal horizon

to keep my eager eyes on
and both ears at once;
plus whatever senses else
close in on whatever befalls
my personal concern's calls
to carefully chosen action
to deal with anything that happens
in whole or in fraction
with what I'm attacked on
to get myself back on
the track for reaction
that will carefully take care of me
from danger to keep myself free.
Precisely, that's the story of me.
Now that you know me, don't you agree?

## FINAL LEAKS FROM THE INK-JOWLED PEN, PRE-COMPUTER STYLE

What words can I still use
to light a meaning-fuse
to decipher what the world still has to say
to me, whose old day
scaringly nears its midnight
and drains out its remaining sight?
What salient form of truth
have I inherited from youth
whose application still applies
from ancient archives of supplies
on shelves in my brain's storage
from early on when I ate my porridge
and then obeyed my parents?
I have a little left, it's apparent,
from youth's full head of bliss
without which living was amiss,
since energy was the breath of me
without which life exacted a steep fee.
The lingering words that I can still use
eke out the waning fuse
of a poetic thank you
to the whole world I was going through
including especially the you and the you
and still more you's from youth

of my store of stockpiled truth
of gratitude for life then.
From the now, I reach out to when,
and extract the juice that I can
with this miserable form of a pen:
The pen with ink in its jowls
that leaks out my late prowls
through all fairs and fouls:
dear old pre-computer,
communication's ancient suitor,
that route of writing letters
to inferiors or betters,
giving time a thorough workout
in the internal-external bout
of what my life's been about,
and raises my whimper to a shout,
that separates now's new from then's when
before I step down into death's den.

# FAMILIARITY WITHIN AN UNEASY DWELLING PLACE

Astonished puzzling grips me.
The lash of wonder whips me.
The dangling cord trips me;
so what solution do you recommend
to the beginning, middle, and end
of this life everybody owns
within his given package of the bones
to flesh himself out with
and construct a character that will fit
in the mental arena in his head?
Don't forget to include the "instead."
A thought eludes me. What is it?
A dream that I got a visit—
From me myself. Oh my!
I thought it was a different guy.

## A LOAD OF FREE ADVICE

You don't have to personally contribute
to evolution, which is its own beaut.
There's so many of us
that if you're childless,
others will take up the slack
and make up for what you lack.
So don't break your back
trying to force out a baby.
Just have fun, and say "maybe."
Maybe you can't afford one, anyway.
So live your own life, and go your own way.
Work for upkeep
but keep up the play.
So to all, "A good day."

# INCENTIVE FOR ACTIVISM

1.

Do you think love conquers all? It conquered me, at least.
I met her at a ball.
She tempted me to be a beast.
I pounced. She pounced back.
How many babies? I lost track.

2.

How love advances evolution
is in the human constitution,
both male and female both.
They take a biological oath
and confirm what Darwin always said.
By coupling in the bed,
evolution will grow a global spread
but don't forget: everyone should be fed.
Whether you wed or not,
starvation is the world's dangerous blot,
so adjust society accordingly
that what we need affordingly
we should all financially get.
Balancing the economy is the big bet.
Or down you go, into the murky wet

where the human race derived
till it's by now so far survived.
But only the lucky few can flourish
by being wealthy enough. The rest perish.

## SAYING MORE THAN I CAN THINK

When life is too much against you,
and the color of your mood is absolutely blue,
don't lose your head and kill yourself.
It's a poor option, despite what you're dealt.
If you keep alive, you have another chance
to get on your high horse and prance.
Your leaping heart will urge its feet to dance.
(Unless your belt snaps, and then you lose your pants.)
Life's notorious ups and downs
reduce us to bewildered clowns,
equally parsing both smiles and frowns,
like women wearing their beauteous halfway gowns
that provoke yea and nay echoing along the parade grounds
and everybody takes a vote
depending on what they emote.
Some comments along life's route—
you can play it arch, or you could play it cute.
If you climb a tree, nibble a fruit
from a convenient twig
that bends itself too big
snappingly. And down you fall to the ground,
break a leg, and be put in harness.
Are we speaking in the right parlance?
I hear you loud and clear
depending on how far, and how near

the obedient sound has to go
from bony elbow to ugly toe
at an extreme pace, or too slow.
Life can be passionately wild, or only so-so.

## **ADVICE TO APPLY. TRY IT.**

A rash impulse that goes too far
may unleash your audacity
to jump into romance's clutches
and hug for dear life unless you drop her
due to the leap you're taking being considered improper.
So imprudent daring has a consequence.
Don't spend loads of dollars for too little pence.
If you err in your actions, make amends
by keeping your emotions short of intense.
Moderation will stop you from making a mistake
and confusing arsenic for a delicious cake
and pursuing a notion that's half-baked.
Moderation is the wisest course.
That's apparently obvious, of course.
If you cook meat, drip it in the right sauce
and let digestion take its burping course
along assimilation's downward route
to cast away the unnecessary
and eliminate what you need to bury.
That's wisdom indeed. Very.

## A PARABLE THAT CAN'T FIND ITSELF

Here's a dilemma, so let's play it.
If you love somebody, it's all right to say it
unless you're already too unrequited.
Then swallow your ill luck, and bite it
till out of it comes a spicy flavor
that introduces forgetfulness. That's a favor.
Then you've lost your love for her.
Thus begins her love for you, in the blur.
If the mouse gives up, then it's time for the cat to purr
& leap to get its prey.
That accounts for the cat's glorious day.
The moral of this? Play it as you may.
A riddle or a puzzle?
You'll find out. Squeeze the nuzzle.
What'll come out? Will it be awful?
How do I know? I'm not resourceful.
Wisdom? I lost it along the way.
When the mouse comes out, the cat is eager to play.

## WHAT WE'RE IN FOR

When evolution occurs, you're in it,
qualified by your automatic birth
to claim your spot on the evolving earth
with a unique identity, that's how you spin it.
Now that you're inside life, go ahead and win it
as a decent human individual
with a bonus for the residual
as a deal-sweetener for extra merit
and all the goods which destiny will inherit
just by luckily being on the spot
and prime negotiations favor your lot.
Hold on dearly for what you've got.
Act coolly, don't disrupt your luck
when the dice scream out that you're hot,
having been a distant visitor
straight from the primeval muck.
Get inside your shelter, which you tuck
on your special sensitive skin
within which, perilously, you spin
from the self-help web
but praying for aid from Good Luck:
that unpredictable substance
in this crucial instance
that closes in, despite your distance
from other historical events

on which you're not specially intent
due to the self-role of your interest.
A good luck plea, feigning
bravado to disguise
your perilous hold on this slippery planet.
It's improvised. No one planned it.
And impossible to understand it;
beyond capability of the intellect
to even ponder, much less detect.
Caught inside life, only death can get you out:
But don't encourage it, keep up with your doubt.
Life's altogether desirable trap
welcomes you, with a brutal slap.
But deftly squirm aside, & beat the rap.

## ABSTRACT TO THE CORE

Life acts in strange ways
radiating from its core.
But where does its core reside?
Slightly a bit on the inside,
but also nudging outside,
splitting the boundaries? So we decide
to make a few rules, and abide.
But we argue on what rules to make.
Supremacy is at stake,
to authentically win, without a fake,
and both sides agree upon it.
Yet neither will give an inch.
My core and I are in a pinch,
or rather an immovable clinch.
Now we have a fundamental clash.
But let definitions set us right.
What do I mean by a "core"?
Is it that which comes before
the remaining part of me,
making the latter inferior?
Or is the whole of me superior?
Does my core even have an interior?
If so, what may such an item be?
I'm a land animal, but I'm at sea
to settle between my core and me.

What do you mean, "core"?
More dispute, and we'll both be a bore
and stumble after or before
the true essence of the inside core.
Oh, to fix this squabble, I'd adore.
But is the balance shifted to the outside?
The fault is these abstractions.
For a cleaner result, consult our actions,
independent of these mutual factions
(broken up into tedious fractions)
in which neither will give an inch.
My impulse now is to painfully pinch
the core I'm angry at. But that's no cinch.
It's bound to pinch back
for the measure of equal vengeance
and so we both sputter our engines,
disputing the very core. But of what?
Mine. But do I have to bear the blame
for my core's internal shame?
We neither have a definite aim
to produce a mutual interpretation
of what definition will do the trick.
Let's find one, or I throw up the whole deal
and of my core I'll cannibal a meal
and throw the bones away
(if bones there be; I'm not sure),
so as to lose the whole fray
and live in the simple light of day.

# SUSPENDED WORDS SLOWLY THAWING ON A HOLIDAY CRUISE

There's a time element here. Malicious gossip, not yet activated, was spoken but not yet spread on a cruise ship by a passenger about other passengers to not-yet-hearing passengers who were in the dark as to what was said due to the frozen arctic temperatures that the ship was slowly passing through, causing the malicious words to be too frozen—dangling in mid-air—to be heard.

Later, when the ship struck milder air on its mid-expensive voyage or cruise, a thaw released the frozen words to melting audibility. Then the dung hit the fan. The now-hearing passengers, to whom the malicious gossip had been intended or directed, were utterly shocked, to even put it mildly, in the milder atmosphere that enabled them to hear and be then outright shocked, as previously alluded to.

While the malicious words were initially in a frozen condition that completely impeded communication during that temporary but suspenseful interlude, the would-be-listeners were in the dark even though it was broad daylight (if the clock, combined with visibility, could be believed).

The release by thawing of the words resulted in the havoc of law suits, complicating a few lives and creating a near-suicide, for whom the weight of doom had descended on a sea holiday.

But here the story has to crawl limply to a premature end, aborted or truncated due in the main to the running out of authorial inspiration in the creative vein. Sorry, folks. But don't consider yourselves deprived in the mystery of the missing ending anticlimactically issued following the dramatic but slow thaw with its subsequent untold revelations, not to mention life-altering consequences. The temptation to go on had to be stoically resisted due to a trip to the bathroom, following which inspiration flagged. My excuse is that brevity is the source of wit, which pervades this ending with tongue-in-cheekiness and a perverse descent of silence that dissipates any further claim to suspense or—in the major—narrative drive.

# A COLLECTION OF UNCERTAIN RECOLLECTIONS, CATEGORICALLY DISORGANIZED

My disorganized brain spreads its memories far apart, so each will have breathing room, unlike a crowded New York subway at the peak crushing hour. But I'd prefer my memories to bunch themselves in tidy packs together, so as best for assembling themselves into pulse-beat rhythms tumbling over each other with the momentum of a momentous moving sequence, like a movie or a successful poem that blazes ahead with brilliant headlights.

At a big party you can see separate conversational groupings or clusters, each person glad and proud to be popular enough to be welcomed to be actively belonging and be seen as such, to avoid a loneliness image.

I'd like to concoct memory patterns, like scrapbooks or photo albums of like-minded memorabilia scraps that fit in to the same squads or squadrons organized along titles of subject matter, time period, social connections, or mood tones; or a humor or heart-breaking theme commemorating being pals, like a bachelor pre-marriage group before wedding bells or baby carriages break up that old gang of mine. Ah, nostalgia!

Or the ballplaying years. Or nights of entertainment spectatorship. Or courtship years buzzing around the spinning web of romance in a heady vortex of passionate funk.

Or the memories so far back they rub tiny shoulders with little burgeoning infantile brains subject to induced memories too vaguely based on uncertain events too early to tell, with teenage maturity too far away to be even a semblance of a problem, just yet.

In old times of war alarm, mobilizing was a problem goal of patriotic entities, accompanied by the rallying songs of those stirring eras of fanatical loyalty to the ranks, to the state; my country is always right.

As it is, when I periodically consult and access my memory box of ill-sorted miscellania, I leap into heaps of free association, like undisciplined hippy "poetry" that scatters itself along surrealistic pretexts that open themselves to "is it art?" debates on sub-amateur levels.

Memories! Oh those golden years! Or those near-death spasms of lifeless depression!

Am I a qualified senile? No, my bee-buzzing memories still sting hard enough to rally me from that singular last-gasp non-art: dementia: with its swift entry to death-rehearsing obliviousness—that negative scattering of falling apart into rubber-limbed baselessness, where memories' solidities aren't even worthy of the bare paper not even or never more written on, take your choice. You're a "were" person.

# LIFE'S TWISTY RHYTHMS

1.

To get comfortable, get upset first,
so that you start at the very worst,
and then, in an accelerated burst,
you're inside a happy reverse
and upset the symptoms of your curse.

2.

With the wind at your back,
you find the right track
and groove up the split rail
to spit on what used to be frail.
You go from where you fail
to where you launch a win;
climb the favorable wind:
Success—can you call that a sin?
Jump off the basement bin.
Otherwise—dear friend, where have you been?
Stay at the place of your conquest
to finally finalize your quest.
You've won. Isn't that the best?
Then you're past needing to pass the test,
my scientific findings do attest.

3.

Finally it's time to celebrate?
You've barely only reached the gate.
Don't be smug and tempt fate.
Certainty? No, it's too late.
Okay, now that you've passed the bar,
don't undo it, all that work to mar.
Don't besmirch your lucky star.
Clutch the high ground where you desperately are.
Don't let it slip away
and impoverish night by losing day.
Halt right there. Be firmly okay.
Confirm your gains. Just stay.
Don't trip from the ground you've won.
Suck down the sweet and honeyed bun
and let it linger in your throat.
Chasing success, don't miss the boat.

4.

That's so proverbial, you can't lose it.
Seeking the plum, don't swallow the pit
where indigestion lurks to drive you into a fit
from which you lose all your gains,
trade them foolishly for your pains.
Now, that's a rotten deal.
In horror, you roar out the worst squeal.

5.

The ups and downs of life, plainly put,
finally shove that unwieldly door firmly shut.
What does that door stand for?
It's a metaphoric symbol. Don't be a bore.

## A MAN'S MANIFESTO

When I'm close to a woman, I feel like a man.
When i get even closer, I feel more mannish.
(When it comes to gender, I think I can manage.)
When I even narrow that gap, I am a man.
But if she ultimately rejects me, manhood has fled
unless I pin her down upon the bed
and our bodies bruise each other, head to head,
till I'm approximately almost dead.
For lust I trade exhaustion instead
and my breathlessness is very manly.
Is there any sperm left? Well, hardly any.
She'll sperm me on, that's uncanny.
There's just some room left, in that ample fanny
to go how many more times? Many.
Enough to provide a full family.
Being manifestly a man
is managing as much as I can,
to the full extent of my span.
Trapped in my cage is an extended man.
Being manifestly a man,
but minus manners,
I do whatever I can
and provide my own answers.
Bring in the burlesque dancers.

## STUDIES IN HUMAN RIVALRY

Being jealous of your serious rivals
for very coveted rewards
is not the way towards
self-respect and happiness.
Maybe I should switch to envy instead?
No. Jealousy and envy are in the same bed.
Both designate you as being in a slump
in the direction of being down in the dump
from which you're too stuck to make a jump
from misery to enlightenment,
to lift your spirits to a heightenment
that indicates a superior mood
to take on your former rivals
and plunge them into envy and jealousy
indicating now they're bad and now you're good,
quite a reversal in your favor
that allows you to gorge on a higher flavor
of whatever life's joyride is in the hay for;
unless you swivel to a sudden detour
that gives you a "loser" image for your neighbor
to fill your life with disrespect
and punish you with his methodical neglect.
Can you battle back with vengeance?
Resort to your slick metal engines

and roar up his despised ass
and knock him dead as you casually pass,
looking back with a bitter laugh
to pound out the rhythm of his epitaph.

## NOTES ON HOW HUMANS MAKE USE OF THE EARTH, OR NOT

Life on earth is not entirely to our satisfaction
any more than we can strike a match on.
Still, what else is there?
Air for our lungs is provided
by quite a clement atmosphere,
so we should hold to the near and dear;
and for our life's sake, we must adhere
to a solid something
provided it doesn't sting
and inject a disease
that leads to our decease,
which is actually our life's opposite,
giving us mental derangement
that makes it difficult to distinguish
between pit and luscious fruit,
between sophisticated life and the savage brute
which except as a baby isn't cute.
Now at dusk, the owl prepares to hoot
and thieves make away with their loot,
under darkness, to the near-by churchyard,
looking for something more nutritious than lard
while criminally marking a playing card.

# **THE GOODS AND BADS OF EVOLUTION**

Evolution is a nice method of staying alive.
All you have to do is join in,
it's been going on a long time
and you were already born a member
so welcome to the human branch
that's already so far advanced.
You were provided with a full set of instincts
and it was easy to learn how to use them.
Don't foul up. Stay on the straight line
and evolution will get you through
though it can't stave off death,
which closes you out, with heart and breath
dysfunctional to say the least.
Evolution: that cruel human beast.

## THE HEEDLESS WORLD LEAVES ME BEHIND

In the murky depths of my past,
did my anticipations grow up to now
in the neat connective sequence?
No, I had no idea
all this would come about
in the outside world, brave and stout.
And me, I've changed too.
Twin growths, the world and me,
keeping each other's easy (?) company,
in a parody of a lockstep.
The world as my lifetime companion
through mountain range and canyon?
But all this was in the city.
The world and I exchanged looks of pity,
and we go on together
through the local climate and weather
at the urban locale
where we kept our weight down with low-cal.
We were each other's pal
like a jolly guy and his strong-willed gal.
We enter the subway
not suspecting the parting of the way.
Had we known, we would have wept
with all our friendship kept.

But while I stop at the local station
and get off in termination,
the world's express keeps blazing ahead
not caring on endless track who's dead.

## YES, BUT

I sing the praises of evolution,
it gives you a free stay in the world
with automatic membership
provided you get born at all.
To evolution I'm in thrall
that even should death befall
me myself as a specimen,
the entire human race
will ride along the wild space
on the friendly turf of the world.
But if I'm dead, include me out.
I can't rejoin. I'm not that stout.
Death expelled me. It's for keeps.
That's the proviso that gives you the creeps
causing widows a wellspring of weeps.
And husbands also cry a lot
when wives get smashed in the same awful blot.

# THE UNDERSTUDY ROLE? NO!

If life sags with disease,
does latent death rehearse to take the stage
with eager replacement of dwindling life,
behind the curtain in nervous readiness
for the understudy role?
Understudy? No, that's the wrong role.
Imagine death trying to portray life!
That's almost criminal casting
and brings perversity to a height,
to sharpen the art of the cartoonist
while elevating satire's savage wit
to pounce on its brilliant new material,
that makes a farce of the great stage:
The saga of the wrong replacement.
A comic defacement
modeling clothes ripped from the basement,
in skull and skeleton's debasement,
which surely was not the case meant.

## PROLONG YOUR STAY

Don't worry about Evolution:
a masterpiece of anti-pollution.
It's here to stay, not gone tomorrow.
So don't begin your sorrow.
You don't even have to contribute
by siring or whelping a new specimen;
you can be a childless bachelor
and still enjoy the free game
by sponging on other people's paternity
and hazardous maternity.
It's there all along for you,
ready to spring aboard
and join intact its generous accord
as a springboard to propel the human race
which nothing and nobody can ever efface
even if thousands of new-fetched bombs
sound all our frantic alarms.
Calm down. Evolution will see you through.
Be passive. Nothing you need to do.
Except to be dead one day
to donate room for many newcomers
to have their turn. It's only fair.
You pre-welcome them aboard
to join in the jolly horde.
But where will you be?

You'll be free with expired membership
whereby you're off the roster
and prolong your lengthy diet of eternal doom
but you won't feel a tinge of gloom.

## FEAR OF CROWDS

I got lost in the crowd
but my soul warned loud,
"Get out of that unruly pack,
get your own self back
from the uncertain anonymity
of lonely self in proximity
to a crowd devoid of name-tags
holding their suitcases or bags."
But in a different set of circumstances
some individuals from that amorphous crowd
could have become my dear buddy friends,
even soul-mates. But that's only speculation.
The crowd compelled my timid hesitation
to introduce myself and shake hands
to casually unchosen members
who might rebuff me and I tremor.
I let that impulse go by
without giving it a try;
my loneliness I'll defy,
its stubbornness prevailed.
So I maintained my fear
of aimless crowds in this northern hemisphere
or wherever they get dangerously near
from that unsafe there
to my secure here.

# FEATURES AND PROBLEMS

An attack of psychology
assaulted the individual.
An attack of sociology
assaulted his community.
An attack of politics
assaulted his whole country,
extending out to the whole world.
An attack of geography
assaulted the anywhere.
An attack of history
assaulted whenever:
and was a matter of time
before the whole world was suffering malaise
and its attending army of distresses
and very poignant excesses.
What could the whole world do?
If it was a cow, it could only moo
and on the juicy cud it must chew;
and do whatever other cows must do
under the friendly assault of the local bull
in nature's realm, bountiful.
And we hope it's also fruitful,
though necessarily brutal.
Some acts, though, fizzle out as futile.
On that note, let's blow our bugle.

## A PRETTY STRANGER EXERCISES HER RIGHT TO REJECT YOU

You used to eye women, ready for a pickup,
in public places where people rove,
like museums or restaurants scattered about
with common access, including conversation
if you dare to intervene another's silence.
Where civic decorum dwells,
passion involuntarily swells
in furtive spontaneous attempt
to chance the sudden moment
with a daring self-introduction
or intrusion on presumed privacy
by witty comment on whatever lady's appearance
is considered a permissive target.
This forced encounter—what's to beget?
A risky foolish stab at romance
heading to an embarrassed regret.
A stranger is free to respond
by denying your proffered bond
as being unseemly abrupt.
Your dastardly move she'll disrupt;
and refuses your offer of a drink or meal.
Now, how you estimate your appeal
has shrunk down low, and you feel

inadequate to the female race
that looks you in the face
with either an amused contempt
or annoyance at your attempt.
You apologize: "It's not what I meant."

## A SEA CATASTROPHE AS A MASS GRAVE FOR THE HUMAN RACE

Life creates an enormous splash
as our human boats cruise to clash
vying for ideal spots of water
in a naval crush of bone-jarring disorder
that wets the participants all
and conduces to their burial fall
in a mass-drowning grave of sogginess
that the sailor victims don't have the foggiest
notion of the nautical disaster
straight from the loins of Neptune's death-master.
Some drowned slowly. Others were faster.

## PROBLEM DIALOGUE

If problems don't get solved, do they fester?

Not always. They can get overlooked and eventually fall off the books.

Okay, I'll put my problems in that category.

You mean your unsolved problems?

Of course. What other?

Some problems require urgent attention quick. To delay would be too late.

You're right. You don't have to provide examples.

Thanks for saving me that trouble.

You're welcome. Let's become friends.

Then do we have to have sex?

No. Is that a problem?

Not necessarily.

Then why bring sex into this?

It's good for publicity.

But this is not an advertisement.

Of course not. But just in case.

# POETRY DIALOGUE

The guy who invented poetry must be a millionaire by now.

I don't doubt it, because there's been lots of practitioners.

Do you include translated poetry?

Sure. Why discriminate?

Do you practice poetry yourself?

No. I'm strictly prose. What about yourself?

Bi-.

What do you mean, "bi-"?

I go both ways.

Okay. That's your poetic license.

# PATENT DIALOGUE

The guy or lady who invented sex—and patented it—he'd be a millionaire by now.

Sure. Sex has really taken off. Without it, where would evolution be?

Your argument is well taken. Evolution would have to be stuck, if sex weren't invented just in time. Now evolution is rampant, and sex's popularity is setting records all over the place. It's gone mad.

You said it. How can we cash in?

We can't. We don't have a case. It's far too late to invent it, being in the popular domain, evolution or no evclution.

Too bad. We're out of luck.

Well, that's the breaks.

## MEMORY DIALOGUE

How can I divide up and rejuvenate my memories before they dry up and die out in advanced old age?

Divide them up? What organizing principles do you use—or are used by? Do you arrange different categories? Do you go by chronological order, or by sentimental emphasis? What memories get periodically reinforced or at least revisited? And what memories get carelessly ignored unless they intrude themselves on an involuntary basis at odd reveries?

Oh, I just want to leave them alone and let them be, to their own devices. I can't exert that much control, so I'll lazily be subject to what offers itself.

Just ease along, right?

Or just let the mind go about things naturally. Maybe a visitation or surprise will pop up and be an inspiration. Some things linger, like regret. Remorse. Triumph. Love. Self-recrimination. Guilt. Loss. Emptiness. Fear. Worry. Depression. Anticipations. Appointments. The ordinary range of consciousness preoccupations. Or just plain fantasy: cloud-gathering and daydreaming. Like going to a movies about which I don't know what to expect, and plunge in to see what happens.

Well, in meandering we've covered enough aspects of this subject.

Sorry. My forgetting has already begun as to what you and I both said.

Short-term memory is your trouble?

Stop analyzing. I'm getting dizzy.

Sleep wouldn't harm you.

It has a lot to feed on. Huge unexplored areas of new vacancy, unplowed in formations of vacant free associations in close tiding to the oblivion's helpless oncoming.

As you lose power, I'll leave you alone. Goodbye.

# THE OPPORTUNITIES OF DONE DUTIES

What do you do with all the extra hours
that hang about? Your duties are over
and bonus time now beckons to you
with leisure delighted to be filled
if you can add to them some strong-willed thrills
and valuable pleasure that you only dreamed about
once stern obligations have been committed
to the put-past and the tempting future looms
trembling with the plea to hurry up
before ordinary modes claim you rigorously
and the simple child disappears vigorously
within the glowing glories of pure waste
that touched the secrets of his unique taste.

## THE MAJOR MATTER, NO MATTER WHAT

The world's here for the asking.
In its radiance I'm basking.
The world is assured of plenty of earth
to slip around on, ever since birth.
Then cut the gloom and take your mirth
into your laughing mouth; or else pout
that death will come: Easy in, easy out.
Transience and brevity: there's the clout
that quite slays us; without a doubt,
time is tragically short.
But comedy prolongs the joy we've brought.
On this issue, the battle is fought.
Can comedy survive tragedy's onslaught?
There's the tussle. In it we're caught.
Ponder it. Nothing's quite naught.
Can an extra year be bought?
At what cost, you old man?
Vigor declines, despite the span
that we can barely extend
to delay the silence that sounds our end.

## INSOLUBLE

Our hopes outstrip their results,
our desires are denied.
Our most cherished wants
sometimes court frustration.
What's a poor man to do?
His problems constitute a whole zoo
that's so mismanaged,
the animals are all outside
and the visitors hemmed in cages.
It's a problem for the ages.

## EVOLUTION VERSUS CIVILIZATION

Evolution is a good idea;
chemically and biologically
it keeps species going on.
That's noble, isn't it?
Not to mention philanthropic
in the very generous sense.
In that case, it makes sense
to praise evolution fully.
Should we also praise civilization
which applies to many a nation?
Yes, it's the human collective,
but with a different perspective.

## KEEP GOING

Life is so exciting, cling to it.
Every ounce of passion, bring to it.
But dullness often intervenes
as many of life's inbetweens.
Life is often a snoring fit
as witness many a boring bit.
Dreary dimness can keep life from getting lit.
But that doesn't mean you should seek an exit
from life's broad potential and merely quit.
Give life a chance to rebound,
and cycle through the stations of its round.
You don't have to be so tightly bound,
so ease your stiffness out and just stick around.
Then you'll live to be longevity's ardent bloodhound.

## WHAT I OWE DARWIN

I rode the many lives before me
to join the evolution parade
as a full-fledged member
in good credit, to remember
to pay my debt to evolution
and preserve Darwin's fame from pollution.
I was able to gain birth
(prelude to life's total totality)
although spoiled by fatality,
since ultimate death is required
by an individual member to be expired
so that evolution itself can live on
based our personal sacrifice upon.
Trust me. This is no con.
I give my life to evolution
as the human race's solution:
Dear Darwin's debt
lest we forget.

## WHY RELIGION TAKES THE SCARE OUT OF LIFE

I come from a long line of evolutionary creatures
who take care of my organs, so do I need preachers
in a perilous world to guarantee safety
and slow down metabolism from life so hasty?
No, but nervousness compels me to seek refuge
from superstitious threats like an enormous deluge
that scares my wits off, death's official prelude
stripping my whole soul down to a damp skeleton
that would empty me of life, and that's no fun.
So you see, preachers are not superfluous.
From holy terror, they have much to do for us.

## BRING IN A PRIEST

Is there a god to welcome our prayers?
We made one up, because we're nervous players
in this private, social game of life
that we can't get through without so much strife
that's so tough to bear, we need a good priest
to bless our thoroughfare through life's feast
so that at the table we're not quite the least
and eat our minimum fare, like a contented beast.

## DEITY'S DESPERATE NEED

God's a vacuum we need to fill
to take the chill out of life's thrill
and so adjust the temperature
that we have guaranteed security in the future
and all our talents are blessed to mature.
We need god to bolster mere nature
that's too insufficient without a deity.
No wonder religion extracts from logic a steep fee
so that from religion's trap we can never twist free.

## A CLERGY MARKET

If I didn't have some clergy, I'd go nuts.
Life is so challenging, it deprives me of guts.
So belief in god is so necessary
to crush all my fears and bury
their residue, and then I'd make merry.
Am I a scared coward? Oh, so very.

## UNCAGED, LOOK FOR DEMOCRATIC FREEDOM

If life gets too exuberant for you,
calm down and go to a peaceful zoo
where the animals are all mild and quiet,
and safely caged, know not to riot.
But do you want to be so subdued,
and trained painfully not to be rude?
Do you need a cage to keep you quiet
when your senses squeeze together in a riot?
Do you want to be confined to a zoo?
The answer of course is a resounding no.
Then leave the zoo and let your exuberance go
in free human life, within society
that allows you democratic freedom and variety.

**SELF-PROTECTION**

Life itself I love to the extreme.
Suicide is my least real dream.
To preserve my life, I take good care
that my nutritional diet is healthy fare,
to keep doctors invisible in their lair
and have no need to lance a cancer bare
or do procedure upon my heart
that would jump my blood pressure to a rocky start.

## NUGGETS FROM LIFE'S WISDOM

On your road through steep longevity's long route,
don't be too risk-taking. Just play it cute.
Eat excellent nutritional meals
to keep you from spinning your wheels.
And if you gamble, seek only the safe deals,
to avoid a long death's anguished squeals.
To test the waters, step gingerly: see how it feels.
Then avoid jumping too quick.
Instead, have yourself a picnic.
Invite of course your friends along
on a selective basis. Then join in a song.

## DECORUM

How carefully to become a gentleman
is the same for becoming a lady:
Be bold and subtle, but not shady.
Be friendly but not too jocular
unless invited to be by the other.
But who might the other be?
His identity is that he's not you.
One man can't add up to two
unless the other one gets included.
Whoever's superior has got to be saluted
even though of not military rank.
Disobey the rules, and then the spank
will have to be administered
but not too fiercely. Who by?
A neutral bystander, that's who.
He knows his place. Do you?

## NAIVETÉ IN ACTION

I've got to tame the world to my needs
by adjusting to the proper creeds
and perfecting the right beliefs
by correcting my wrong disbeliefs
to fall in line with everyone else
although they harbor disparate notions
and form a coalition of disagreements
bewildering to figure out whose side to be on.
Well, I have a sure assortment of choices.
I'll raise all my multiple voices
to make a safe world for democracy
to pull our citizens together
to set a model standard
for all other countries to abide
and to co-operate, not to divide.
Oh this universe, so sweetly wide.
Let my thought with others coincide
to form the cosmic illusion of a uniform side.
I'm composing an ideal
far as yet from completing the real.

## HOW TO PREPARE

Please, world, spare me from delirium.
Give me a vial of pure serium
to balance my equilibrium.
On you, world, I wish to get a grip
before my senses split apart and rip.
Is homeostasis within my ken?
I'll sign up for it, if I can
and refer to it, now and then,
especially if I'm in trouble.
Then of doses I'll take a double
and clean the debris of my rubble.
I'll shave my skin of excess stubble
to make my wife and me a perfect couple.

# A DUBIOUS ADVERTISEMENT FOR COUNTRY LIVING

Not everybody lives in a city.
For them, compassion requires a pity.
They're stuck in the old remembered hills
and such boring places against their wills.
They don't have the consolation of skyscrapers
to block out the dull abandoned sun
in empty valleys where neighbors are sparse
and the only amusement is farming the land
with relentless toil while a cow looks on
and boring rain is the only view to look upon
or maybe a deserted swan in a near-by brook.
Big cities spawn the action of a crook
and the cops who resist him all day long,
while country living doesn't even deserve another look
and hillbillies on a harmonica have to play their own song
in pitiful isolation for the lack of action
except occasionally there may be a horse transaction
and no newspaper to even analyze it.
Occasionally you hear a train whistle
rolling by with nowhere to stop.
Country children don't even have a school to go to
except so many miles away, it's not worth it.
The whole population of country living
amounts to the occasional hay-nibbling imbecile

whose only schooling happened to be A-B-C
in a one-roomed shack
right beneath a haystack.
In rural life what you get is plenty of lack
that shows the uneducated slack
of nowhere to return to if you have to look back.
While cities at least have gunfire
from which you can amusingly expire.

# THE WORLD AS OUR LANDLORD. BENEVOLENT? NOT ALWAYS

I credit the world for being the location
of all of my life's activities, every one.
All within the radiance of our sun.
The world can never take a vacation
from being my tried and true landlord.
On his property, I try not to be bored.
Do I have to pay rent? Oh plenty.
Life is not an eternal picnic, you see.
If you're behind in rent, can you get off with a plea?
That depends on the law of justice, you see.
Real estate creates a whole lot of wealth
from the landlord's side, but not to the tenant.
But is the world a tenement house?
No, it contains gold and riches.
An owner's wives can be rich bitches.
Poverty is created by being evicted.
Your possessions are thrown out in front
even though it cruelly rains.
The landlord reigns, and he hires a bailiff.
If the tenant complains, he's set on by a mastiff
whose surly bark is louder than his ominous sniff.
Always be a man of property,
and the law is on the side of your propriety.
You own the whole deal, entirely.

Let the evicted tenant go out expiredly
with wife and children and drenched suitcases.
Is the world accountable for this cruelty?
No, just the evil landlord
whose charge of rent exceeds what you afford,
so you lose the residence you so adored.
That's where poverty comes to be so abhored
that people protest a rent increase
that causes their extra capital to decrease.
Landlords on this world, unite!
You have nothing to lose but your tenant's right:
He may be wronged, but to you it's perfectly right.

## THE SWOON OF THE SELF-LOST

Oh, all that I am or ever was
are brought together in a confusing buzz
that separates things that are too alike
and tells the rest to take an interminable hike
along the roads on foot or bike.
Do I know even what life is?
I melt down before that ardent quiz
and modestly defend myself: "I'm no whiz."
Life then gives me a reassuring pat
on my weak back, and I fall flat.
From that position I have no clue: "Where am I at?"
The world is a fine and foreign place
where I've lost my soul and find no grace.

## NO TRANSLATION

Here I am. Hello, life.
We've been together for so long
but have never been properly introduced.
I find you breathtaking and am seduced.
Life replies in a foreign voice:
"Go through the motions and rejoice
that you just exist
however surrounded by a mist.
Now I'm lost. Where are you?"
But I didn't understand the language.
We're separated. I languish,
divided by my own life
because our tongues are unalike.

## GIVE UP? SHAME ON YOU

This world has so many aspects,
it's so complicated, that some people defect
from problems too compelling, and dive off
by taking a self-defeating
route to a most embarrassing suicide
because confronted with a problem they couldn't decide
what to do about, they just ruled themselves out.
Their social status took a deep dive
by no longer boasting themselves alive.
Their survivors hope to continue to thrive
and if a bachelor, quickly wive.
And if a woman, grab a husband quick
better the jitters to lick.

## HURRY UP TO STOP

Life could go all over the place,
but that's too much, try to discipline it,
otherwise you'll be the victim of a fit
that doesn't know enough what to omit
and has to undergo slippage of your wit.
So instead of going all over the place,
become modest and just know your place
and narrow down before your weirdness makes a case
that you're too unfit to even live longer
and that it's impossible for you ever to go wronger
and so tune out the melody of your songer.

## **DIPPING AND DROWNING IN THE SEA OF OTHERS**

The world is full of people. That's the hazard.
People? I'm one of them myself.
So if they're a problem for me, so am I to them.
I handle each person one at a time
depending on what's going on between us
both for the pros and cons.
Do we like each other or not? And to what degree?
Is social life endless negotiations,
sorting out envy and comparing each other
and to whose advantage when?
Some friends I like better than others,
but is my evaluation reciprocated?
These are delicate matters but need not be.
Navigate the sea of people,
and such they do to me.
We end up with marriage partners
and friends to various degrees,
also colleagues in the field of work,
and neighbors, making for convenient geography.
Remember, I'm one of them.
How do they see me,
starting up from indifference?
Intrigues and mixed feelings
all along our endless dealings

with others just like us or almost,
and who's the humble one, and who's the boast?
And who's the quicker to turn up his ghost
and disappear from the rest of the throng?
and by morality, who's right and wrong?
Who pulls his weight too much,
and others such?
Oh the eerie social song:
a whole mixed chorus.
But please—don't bore us.
Don't be against—be for us.
And if we fall, restore us.

## ADDRESS TOPIC: HOW DOES THE WORLD FARE?

Men and women: there's an intrigue right there.
Gender separation brings on attraction
and other permutations of body attitudes
with accusations and gratitudes.
The fur flies and so do everything else
when the tensions start to pull in
or antagonistically fall out,
creating a whole mixture of emotions
backed up by endless notions
and sparking a stack of motions
dragging along behind them
the casualties and their effects.
Loads of blame, and lots of suspects.
Deal love into the pack of cards
and that's a potent factor.
We participate—we're the actor.
Except that it's a real role
playing the high-stakes game
and the gambling tensions mount high.
It's unbearable, yet we get by
by time's dividing the action
and delaying, and forcing the issue.
Oh, we're in it all right,
up to the full extent
tempering with merriment
the utter serious matters

on which we're expert chatters
and well analyze the points
to steady aright the loosening joints
and hold the structure together.
We're part of society.
It's not presumptuous to simply join
and place our money on the current coin.
Fashions flurry in and out,
hold on, and hold stout.
Here's the train ride to where?
In some cases, suicide,
and all else beside.
We scramble, slip, and slide,
once the train will next arrive.
We get out and dip and dive
in weakness or the strength to strive,
and maintain our right to stay alive.
The police will repair the damage in any dive,
arrest the wrong ones, and ignore the others.
Unrelated, we're sisters and brothers
in a broken up family
that divides up the damages and pays.
Work and play, on endless days
while social fabric frays
on a world managing to slip by
and hold high up the neutral sky.
Our exclamation? "Oh my!"

## **THE PUBLIC'S VERDICT—IS THAT WHAT LIFE COMES DOWN OR UP TO?**

Is life the question? Or the mere detail of digestion?
Life is the glowing amplitude within which small things exist
that loom momentous to us, if you thus persist.
The essential primal thing of course is to exist.
That's the thing you explore and exploit with each fist.
I can draw you a lengthy list of what's entailed
and you'll find that every item there is much detailed,
and the road to success is paved with what failed.
Some truths slip away, others are nailed
by the carpenter of life who's called mere Chance.
Does he play choreographer to life's fitful dance?
How can I tell? I'm only taking a glance
and making pompous conclusions from it,
trying to insert some evidence of wit
to firm the throne or stool on which reputation
stands in good stead or not with the public
and whether their admiration is a wisp or will it stick?
Now I close shop, and with it my rhetoric
asking whether "good" or "bad" is the verdict you pick.
If it's in the negative, you upset digestion and make me sick.

## WHY THE NOW AND THEN IS PREFERABLE TO THE ALL AT ONCE

Life implores you to live it up.
Watch out, though. It's like a time bomb
which in the midst of your belly, could explode
and expend your whole load
of excessive passion,
unlike the usual fashion
of playing it ultra safe
and calming down your nerves
by modestly playing the middle course
and diluting somewhat your entire force
to have some of it left over
in safe reserve, to use again
along the safety rhythm of now and then.
(Need help? I'll tell you "when.")
Leave the all at once to another day,
as you alternate your daily rule of work and play
with leftover's utmost strength
to ration out your limit-prone length.

## UNCOMFORTABLE. (THE RIGHT TO BE SHY)

When I live in the world, is it like wearing clothing?
My clothing is outside my skin; the world is outside my
 clothing.
But what if I'm both nude and naked,
with no clothing to intervene?
Then the world is more closely or tightly outside of me,
me, meaning my unclothed body.
"Now I'm suddenly shy and must leave this poem
because too much lewdness is exposed
directly before the reader—
too close to home,
too shocking and outrageous;
all my puritanical instincts are aroused
and not even spoused.
Excuse me. Goodbye."
Now begins the aftermath:
justifying my right to flee
and not having to pay a fee.
Go empathize with me.
Let's be free to be shy
under the timid protection of the sky.
And from the ground up, the earth is there
to stall off people's uncouth glare
at my clotheless human form
casually close to the acceptable norm.

## THE TUNE-LADEN BIRD

Life is sometimes too much for me.
I've got to jump and jive free.
Then I calm down again
and take a breather and go to sleep…
Until a little bird shall peep
outside the window, "Get up, you jerk.
It's time for you to get back to work.
The boss fires layabouts who shirk."
"Okay bird, thanks for your advice.
But no thanks for rousing me: that's your vice,
if you want me to spell it out precise.
Now go fill your appetite with a bunch of lice."
Protesting the bird's simultaneously harmful help
whose untimely tune wrenched me to a yelp,
made me at least get to work on time
to earn my squalid nickels and my total dime,
and furnished me with the inspiration to rhyme
by compounding like-sounding vowels to rhythms prime
and withdrawing me from this seedy world gripped with
    grime
that demoralizes us to attitudes soft on crime.

## ALL ABOUT MOST EVERYTHING, JUST ABOUT

History has arrived at a new juncture
where the past is put up to puncture.
Time allows the new to replace the old
with its propensity to be bold.
Please let our delicate fabric hold
and disarray itself for the new mold
which as yet goes on untold.
Oh it's good to be alive
with interesting times ahead.
Let's consume our bottles of wine
and the magical grains of daily bread.
Our finances have set our overhead
but we duck under and get the job done instead.
Evolution has forced us to breed
and current philosophy gives us our creed.
Matters of health direct our feed
by the graces of medical science.
Let's shout our ways through the empty silence
and live despite the plunging finance.
Let's curtsy and twist at the folk dance
and take our aggressive stance
to snap up a mate to support evolution,
with infants crawling on the earth's surface
with extra collective purpose.

Our anarchy undergoes stern organization
to drive the world on, plus our nation.
We aim for peace, to justify agitation,
and conduct our services at the same old station.
Hence the plea for a little more patience.
We break apart into the new elation.

# THIS WAS ACTUALLY BROADCAST?

"The world does a great job containing life
and life does a great job filling the world,
so congratulations are equally due to both of them,
and both take their places nicely
within the even broader scope of the universe
which is grandiose enough to accommodate
the world and its multibilities of lives
all active and at the same time grappling
with the problems that crop up throughout the course of events.
Any more commentary on these matters
is later covered on our next broadcast,
so tune in we beseech you,
especially where our sponsors are concerned,
whose interest is industriously financial
despite what the news happens to be or not.
In conclusion, I leave you, to take care of my brain clot."

## BOASTING TOWARD ADMIRATION

Interpeople acts—they're intriguing.
So many occur, but it's not fatiguing
to get such interesting gossip
of how people slide and slip
trying from each other to win
true admiration and then to spin
such interchanges to boast about it
and then to present themselves with a toast about it
to win extra admiration from bystanders
who try to be understanders
of how wonderful the boasters are
with reputations no one can mar.
But boasting can only go so far.
You've got to prove yourself to everyone.
You've got to improve every tale you've spun
not only to be admired, but to make it fun.
And getting endorsement from other admirers too
so that the whole world is just your oozing, purring zoo
whose dissenters number astonishingly few.
From such a reputation up high,
you hear a chorus of echoes building up to the sky,
all happy to belong to your fan club,
eager to polish your apple with an extra rub.

## AMBITION'S SOCIAL ULTIMATE

From other people I want approval,
and not a consensus for my removal.
I want everybody not only to love me
but to rank absolutely nobody above me.
I want to prove how marvelous I am
so that from my concert nobody will exit and scram.
I want the whole world not only to give a damn
but to give me everything they own also.
If they don't, it will come as a considerable blow.
In comparison with me, everyone will rank below
and warm themselves at the feet of my numinous glow,
daring the negligible arrival of any foe
to threaten my supremacy with even a tinge of woe.
This guarantees my social success. Just so.

# MUTUAL CURE

1.

My loved one and I had a dispute.
Unjustly, she called me "brute."
But then I took her out to sup
where with food dangling on the lip
we kissed the food away and made up,
soon to celebrate with a noisy sip
of real red wine that tore into our gut
and sealed our reunion divinely shut.

2.

How our bad mix found a fix
was the blessing then, and hope it sticks,
so that our only kicks will be on the bed
where our lovely future children are now being bred.

## MARITAL DISPUTE APPEASED

Should my love and I part angrily
and the bitter blows come down to strangle-ly,
let's stop it and start a family soon
from half past bedtime to the hour of high noon,
a marathon breathlessly taken to swoon
over the action's outcome dangle-ly.
Thus it depends
on how it ends,
the ends that shall crucially meet
and the meat's bone is tortuously sweet.

## TERM IT TRAGEDY TO FORCE BLAME OUT

Am I the victim of tragedy?
Not if I use the right strategy.
Tragedy is when it's not your fault
that your happiness is stalled,
because circumstance is called
responsible, not you, for bad news.
So you see, you're excused.
You're lucky, no blame is cast
on your accidental shoulder
for misfortune's sordid blast.
Onward, stalwart soldier.
March proud, march bolder.
Dial your fortitude colder.
Insert misery into its locked-up past.
Let "survivor" belong truly
to your whole history, unruly.

## TWO OLD CELEBRITIES

Posthumously, of course, was Darwin jealous
that Edison's invention was more to the point
than Darwin's mere discovery?
One made light illuminate the dark,
to a literal practical degree,
an actual invention very concretely.
The other made an intellectual discovery
fact by fact pointing out the process.
But the bulb at that time was still in the dark,
unfulfilled of its future radical spark.
When Edison said, "Let there be light,"
he proved proverbially that he was right,
igniting the moonless night
and reversing its visible blight.
Poor Darwin was left behind
to toil by the miserable sun, practically blind.
Finally, it was Edison's turn,
to make Darwin jealously burn.
Both, though, put in a valid claim
for commendably justified fame,
taking diverse chronological paths
to methodically do the maths
required by their separate tasks.
"Can posterity do more?" one asks.
"No," is our joint reply.

"Invention has done its duty,
and mere discovery did what it could.
In our computer age,
we've gone beyond wood
or the car's reversible hood."
A plunge into comparative history
partially eases its mystery
if treated wistfully.

## THE UNTIRING FLAVOR OF A WORD FAVORITE

"Love" is the world's broadest cliché.
Can it still be used freshly? It may.
That's because its lengthy meaning is here to stay.
And for variations, listen to what people say
along yesterday's long road, and past today,
requiring evolution to pick up sparks along the way
to ignite further firecrackers in full fray,
a fiery path of stampeding glory
adding love's roving sound to the ever bonding story,
continuously linking pairs and pairs galore
to rich humanity's historical store.
Need I emphasize further? But I'm no bore.

## THE CURATIVE ANESTHESIA

This world once got my number.
It used to shock me, but now I'm number.

*A Tribute to M.C., by Peter Jackson*

## A WESTWARD NEW YEAR MESSAGE TO MARVIN

Once, beset by destiny and lumbago,
I consulted a psychic physiotherapist,
(An experience not to be missed—
you get two payoffs for one charge
when the medium is the massage.)
So nowadays my spine is fine
And my esprit is quite divine.

But that was all a while ago;
today there is a cuter medication
for moral-corporeal declination.
By polar airwaves (or is it subatlantic cables?)
come Marvin's magic hermeneutic fables,
despatched from Hudson east to Thames
as tasty victuals for his English friends.

What's not to like? Give them a go,
they're not at life's expense, they're free,
they tackle the big things that end in 'e'
(mortality, sexuality, society, identity, matrimony, and then
    there's 'e'volution—
with Darwin as the top Marvinian solution);
they blend the deftness of a Shakespeare sonnet

with homely adages a fortune cookie paper might have on it.

To call a halt to this farrago,
like Father Time I now distribute
an undeservedly missed tribute.
Among our poets there's no better man
than the crafty Betjeman,
(like you, with rhymes he had a lot of fun,
though he was less addicted to the pun);
his Indian summer was a golden spell,
a lap of honour (or the final bell?).
<u>Late-flowering lust</u>\* shows literary senescence
that's anything but lyric obsolescence;
[\*the first poetic hyperlink?—just double-click it,
you can do it, as you did with cricket.]
But JB's perpetual antiquarianism
lacked your habitual optimism
for which (to mix a sporting metaphor)
the pitcher's richer and the batter's better for.
So play your shots profusely round the clover
until the umpire calls the over over,
and stretch your innings—live to be a million
before you climb the steps of that pavilion!

---

\*http://www.johnderbyshire.com/Readings/latefloweringlust.html

Photo by Maggie Beale

Marvin Cohen is an American essayist, novelist, playwright, poet, humorist, and surrealist. He is the author of nine published books and several plays. His short fiction and essays have appeared in more than 80 publications, including *The New York Times*, *The Village Voice*, *The Nation*, *Harper's Bazaar*, *Vogue*, *Fiction*, *The Hudson Review*, *Quarterly Review of Literature*, *Transatlantic Review*, and *New Directions* annuals. His 1980 play *The Don Juan and the Non-Don Juan* was first performed at the New York Shakespeare Festival as part of the Poets at the Public Series. Staged readings of the play have featured actors Richard Dreyfuss, Keith Carradine, Wallace Shawn, Jill Eikenberry, Larry Pine, and Mimi Kennedy. Born in Brooklyn in 1931, Cohen has described himself as one who has "risen from lower-class background to lower-class foreground." He studied art at Cooper Union but left college to focus on writing, supporting himself with a series of odd jobs including mink farmer and merchant seaman. He also taught creative writing at The New School, the City College of New York, C.W. Post of Long Island University, and Adelphi University. Cohen currently lives in New York City with his wife, a retired paperback editor.

www.ingramcontent.com/pod-product-compliance
Lightning Source LLC
Chambersburg PA
CBHW020925090426
**42736CB00010B/1047**